Treasures of the American Arts and Crafts Movement

1890-1920

Tod M. Volpe ∎ Beth Cathers

Treasures of the American Arts and Crafts Movement

1890-1920

Text by
ALASTAIR DUNCAN

Introduction by
LESLIE BOWMAN

HARRY N. ABRAMS, INC.,
PUBLISHERS, NEW YORK

*We have dedicated this book to Vance Jordan, Carol Bohdan
and David Cathers*

*For if it were not for their love, support, and guidance this book would not have
been written and our lives would not be what they are today*

Special acknowledgments to Meagan McKearney

Library of Congress Cataloging-in-Publication Data

Volpe, Tod M.
  Treasures of the American Arts and Crafts Movement.

  Bibliography: p.
  Includes index.
  1. Decorative arts—United States—History—19th century.
  2. Decorative arts—United States—20th century.   3. Arts and
  crafts movement—United States.
I. Cathers, Beth.   II. Title.
NK807.V65   1987   745'.0973   87-1120
ISBN 0-8109-1695-9

Published in 1988 by Harry N. Abrams, Incorporated, New York

A Times Mirror Company

Printed and bound in Italy

Contents

1 Furniture

2 Ceramics

3 Metal and Silver

4 Lighting and Windows

5 Miscellaneous

Prefaces

A Time for Change

TOD M. VOLPE

Treasures of the American Arts and Crafts Movement is both timely and significant. It is, first and foremost, a beautifully conceived art book, yet there is a deeper meaning to its creation and the objects it illustrates. This has to do with the concept of duality that exists not only in art, but also in life. It has to do with what is seen, and what is not seen; with appreciation and reappreciation; with birth, rebirth, and the renewal of our values – of hope and love and spirit.

It is no concidence that this book comes into being approximately one hundred years after the birth of the Arts and Crafts style and philosophy for living. The setting today is very much the same as it was then. People are searching for something new and revitalizing. Now, as in the past, there is a great need for a better understanding of the meaning of life, of the nature of things, and of man's relationship to the universe and to himself. It is time now, as it was then, for all of us to examine our lives, to consider how we relate to ourselves and to each other, and how we can best use our individual creative gifts in our daily existence. The way we have been living and the way we have perceived the world are no longer of value either to ourselves or to the general health and welfare of our planet and all its life forms.

It is the dawn of a new age, a time to reconstruct and a time – especially – to redefine our goals; to heal ourselves and begin anew. We are at a crossroads, perhaps the most important in the history of our world. We have the power to create anything we desire, or, with the very same power, to destroy ourselves and everything around us.

Great changes are taking place, similar to those experienced in their time by Stickley, Hubbard, Wright, and their contemporaries. Our lives must also change. We must realign ourselves to honest values and *enjoy* – in an extraordinary way – the ordinary, simple aspects of life. It is time, without losing a sense of balance, to look at the connections between art and life, nature and industry. Perhaps through re-evaluation and understanding – brought about by the art, ideals, and approach to life of our forbears – we shall discover a mode of existence that is in harmony with our natural environment, and a way to appreciate, to a greater degree, the art we love and the lives we live. The artists of the American Arts and Crafts Movement believed art and industry could work together; believed, too, that people should not compete with Nature, but should understand and respect it. They hoped that through their work people would come to value the beauty of the world around them and by so doing would come to love each other, themselves, and all living things.

Today we are faced with a decision: Do we continue on the same road, or do we accept the challenge for change? For me, change is what this book is about. *Treasures of the American Arts and Crafts Movement* is about transformation.

We have selected works of art not simply for the exquisiteness of their use of the medium, but also for the sources from which they draw their inspiration. We have chosen pieces which represent the high point of the creative experience. Each piece – whether it be ceramics, furniture, silver, or other form – is a *tour de force* which will in itself help people to comprehend the tremendous devotion and labor that was necessary to bring these pieces to fruition. Perhaps we can then begin to apply the same devotion and industriousness to our own art and our own lives. Hopefully we can begin to understand the creative process which each of us has the potential to use in our daily lives.

It is not just the skillful mastery of technique that brought these forms to life. There is without question something greater – an inner connection which allows these artist/ craftsmen to relate to their art with a revitalizing sense of realism and a fresh imagination. There is commercialism here, but if we look closely we can see something else. There is an underlying force which has brought all of this, as all creative endeavors, to the surface – a power that brings joy, happiness, and excitement to both the creator and the admirer. That power is love.

For me, this book has been a labor of love, and I trust that each person who discovers it and is nourished by the objects it illustrates will feel that love and carry it into the world around them.

I wish personally to thank Kristin Elizabeth Hein for loving me and teaching me how to share; Vance Jordan, my cousin and my friend for giving me the opportunity to grow; Beth Cathers, my partner and co-author, Meagan McKearney, my assistant and my guardian angel, Alastair Duncan and Stanley Baron, for enabling this book to be created, Thelma and Irving Sherman, Arlene and Robert Kogod, Judith and Tom Dillenberg, Gloria and Richard Manney, Lois and Ira Kay, Barbara and Jack Hartog, and Marcia and William Goodman for their friendship, love, and support, and everyone else who contributed to this project and to the growth of the Jordan-Volpe Gallery.

I would especially like to thank Robert Blasberg who helped me build my first bridge, Joel Silver and Darrel Couturier who helped me find another world to extend it to, and Jack Nicholson, a very special soul in the Universe, to whom I am grateful for much more than I can express.

Most important, I wish to thank God and the Universe for helping to guide me and find the strength and instincts to fulfill my destiny, and my Mother and Father for bringing me into this remarkable world.

The Meaning of the American Arts and Crafts Movement in Our Own Time

BETH CATHERS

What does it mean to be at home in the twentieth century? The fact is, a fundamental sense of discomfort and displacement permeates our everyday lives. This feeling of alienation is no less disconcerting now than it was when it first began. Prior to the modern predicament, man tilled the soil, worshipped his God and knew his place in the overall scheme of things. A comforting sense of rootedness nourished his soul. However, this feeling of place underwent a radical transformation. The confident belief that values rested on a firm foundation was replaced by the uncanny suspicion that tradition was in fact groundless.

Two divergent responses emerged out of this growing awareness. One, nihilism, sought actively to deconstruct all traces of lingering belief in any foundation which provided man with solace and orientation. It exposed values as illusions designed to protect man from the recognition of his own condition. Man's nature is revealed as homeless. Living truthfully in the twentieth century means living with homelessness, however uncomfortable this may be.

The second response, like the first, accepted the failure of traditional values. But it did not resign itself to characterizing the nature of man as homelessness. Rather, it held open the possibility for man to be at home in the world in a truly modern way.

This response unearthed new or perhaps long forgotten experiences of meaning. Deep and satisfying but buried feelings began to stir in the void left by the crumbling of traditional foundations. These feelings opened onto a sense of beauty found present in the very fabric of the everyday world. They made possible a new and strictly modern sense of nourishing rootedness which had its source in a heightened sense of a beauty which is embedded in the world itself. And the latter led to a transformation in the nature, and the very meaning, of being at home. Living in close proximity to these intrinsic meanings was a path leading back into an authentic way of being human.

The American Arts and Crafts Movement addressed, in this second way, the unsettling modern issue of man's place in the world. However, dealing with the situation required the forging of a new vocabulary. For American artists and craftsmen, the machine held open new possibilities for returning man to a sense of being at home. It enabled the production of forms which grew in a straightforward way out of an understanding of function and materials. Applied surface ornament, like the traditional values it reflected, came to be seen as obscuring rather than enhancing what was truly beautiful. Instead, a sense of beauty was achieved which emanated from precise proportion, fine construction, and the choice of material. An object produced in this way opened up a view into itself, allowing itself to be seen as itself, to shine forth in all its inherent warmth and simple splendor. Well-proportioned forms grew organically from a clean and direct expression of function, structure, and the nature of material; the result was that the new objects brought man back in touch with himself.

Objects of the American Arts and Crafts Movement were treasures intended for everyday use. Thus man's involvement with them could take place in a familiar and intimate way. Their meaning, however, is not reducible to mere function. Like constellations which can be used to navigate, the beauty of their presence vastly overflows any function they may have. It is a beauty which leads man back along a path to himself. Involvement with objects of the American Arts and Crafts Movement is not a retreat into the fantasy of a nostalgic past. Rather, it retrieves the possibility of allowing man to live close to a primordial sense of beauty. It is by living in an intimate manner with this sort of presence that man can continue to feel himself at home in the twentieth century.

Introduction

LESLIE BOWMAN

The Arts and Crafts Movement in the United States was responsible for sweeping changes in attitudes towards the decorative arts, then considered the minor or household arts. Its focus on decorative arts helped to induce American museums and private collectors to begin collecting furniture, glass, ceramics, metalwork, and textiles in the late nineteenth and early twentieth centuries. The fact that craftsmen, who were looked on as mechanics or artisans in the eighteenth century, are frequently considered artists today is directly attributable to the Arts and Crafts Movement. The importance placed on attractive and harmonious home decoration is also traceable to this period, when Victorian interior arrangements were revised to admit greater light and more freely flowing spaces.

The American Arts and Crafts Movement, like its British model, reacted against mechanized processes that threatened handcrafts and resulted in cheapened, monotonous merchandise. Founded in the late nineteenth century by British social critics John Ruskin and William Morris, the movement revered craft as a form of art. In a rapidly industrializing society, most Victorians agreed that art was an essential moral ingredient in the home environment, and in many middle- and working-class homes craft was the only form of art. Ruskin and his followers criticized not only the degradation of craftsmen reduced to machine operators, but also the impending loss of daily contact with hand-crafted objects, fashioned with pride, integrity and attention to beauty. In 1861 William Morris founded one of the first companies devoted to providing simple, handcrafted furniture; other craftsmen's guilds followed, and the movement took its name from the Arts and Crafts Exhibition Society, founded in London in 1888.

In the United States as well as in Great Britain, reformers extolled the virtues of handcrafted objects: simple, straightforward design; solid materials of good quality; and sound, enduring construction techniques. These criteria were interpreted in a variety of styles, ranging from rational and geometric to romantic or naturalistic. Whether abstract, stylized, or realistically treated, the consistent theme in virtually all Arts and Crafts design is nature.

The Arts and Crafts Movement was much more than a particular style; it was a philosophy of domestic life. Proponents believed that if simple design, quality materials and honest construction were realized in the home and its appointments, then the occupants would enjoy moral and therapeutic effects. For both craftsman and consumer, the Arts and Crafts creed was seen as a talisman against the undesirable effects of industrialization: political corruption, the exploitation of labor, urbanization, immigration, and the factory system.

The most prominent figure in the American Arts and Crafts Movement was Gustav Stickley (1857–1942). After visiting C.F.A. Voysey and other British Arts and Crafts designers on a trip to England, Stickley founded his own company in 1899, devoted to producing Arts and Crafts furnishings. Located near Syracuse in Eastwood, New York, the United Crafts (renamed the Craftsman Workshops in 1904) produced furniture, metalwork, lighting, and textiles. For the company trademark, Stickley chose "*Als ik kan*",[1] the Flemish version of William Morris's motto, "Si je puis," meaning "if I can," and signifying the efforts of the craftsman. Stickley explained his goals as follows:

The United Crafts endeavor to promote and to extend the principles established by Morris, in both the artistic and the socialistic sense. In the interests of art, they seek to substitute the luxury of taste for the luxury of costliness; to teach that beauty does not imply elaboration or ornament; to employ only those forms and materials which make for simplicity, individuality and dignity of effect.[2]

In 1901 Stickley began to edit and publish *The Craftsman*, a journal which became the single most important factor in popularizing Arts and Crafts principles throughout the United States. Stickley included philosophical as well as practical treatises on the meaning and implementation of the Arts and Crafts lifestyle in America. So successful were both his journal and his company, that the term "craftsman" was popularly used to refer to the Arts and Crafts style.

Stickley enjoyed national success. His mail-order catalogues reached every part of the country, and showrooms from Boston to Los Angeles displayed his lines. Soon his designs began to be copied and frequently downgraded by furniture companies throughout America. To keep his own costs reasonable and meet the enormous middle-class demand, Stickley employed machinery. He believed that it relieved craftsmen from monotonous labor and permitted them to concentrate their valuable skills on the more important details. With few exceptions, this viewpoint characterized the American Arts and Crafts Movement in

Right

iv   *Photo portrait (c.1910) of Gustav
Stickley, the designer most responsible for the
dissemination of Arts and Crafts principles
throughout America, and the country's most
successful creator of Arts and Crafts
furniture.
Courtesy Tod M. Volpe*

practice, if not always in rhetoric, and distinguished it from the British movement. On the whole, American proponents believed that mechanization needed to be guided and controlled, not avoided.

Stickley eventually overextended his financial empire and was forced to declare bankruptcy in 1915. A year later he published the final issue of *The Craftsman*. The Craftsman Workshops were taken over by his brothers' rival firm, L. & J.G. Stickley, also of Syracuse. The latter firm had long imitated Stickley's designs, but after 1916 focused increasingly on colonial revival styles.

Most of Stickley's furniture is minimal and rectilinear in design, emphasizing its materials and construction. In the absence of applied decoration, the projecting tenons and keys, slats, spindles, paneled sides and supportive brackets become decorative as well as functional elements (ills. 2, 12). The floriform table (ill. 1) contrasts with most Craftsman furniture, and represents a rare and early appearance of the Art Nouveau style in Stickley's work.

Stickley's use of wood, construction techniques, and certain forms was influenced by seventeenth-century American colonial furniture. In common with early New England furniture, Stickley favored quarter-sawn oak and joined or framed construction.[3] Like early colonial furniture, Stickley's forms were squatter and more human in scale than those of Georgian or Victorian furniture. Thick, riven oak boards and joined construction produced heavy case pieces. Stickley undoubtedly preferred the scale of joined furniture, and also the additional strength of these methods. Oak is one of the strongest woods, and the riving method increases resistance to warpage and shrinking. Joined construction utilizes the strongest furniture joint, the mortice and tenon, while the panel and frame method permits the wood to expand and contract without stressing its construction.

Like early New England chairmakers, Stickley favored stretchers joining the legs, and leather upholstery with brass tacks. Stickley's low-backed leather dining chairs closely copied seventeenth-century examples (ii, iii), while his tall, spindle-backed seating forms (ill. 12) related to early eighteenth-century banister-back chairs (i). Other early colonial forms in Stickley's repertoire were trestle and gate-leg tables, chests, joint stools, and settles. A hall seat (ill. 4) was directly inspired by early eighteenth-century high-backed settles.

In 1903, Stickley hired architect-designer Harvey Ellis (1852–1904) to design furniture, house plans, and house interiors for illustration in *The Craftsman* and in Stickley's architectural publication, *Craftsman Homes*. While respecting the structural dominance of Stickley's forms, Ellis introduced 'arching curves and subtle ornament that softened the sharp rectilinear quality of Craftsman furniture (ills. 6, 8). Some of his inlaid designs are related to motifs in the works of the Scottish designer Charles Rennie Mackintosh. Ellis's untimely death in 1904 cut short the successful design relationship.

The medieval influence apparent in British Arts and Crafts was largely absent in Stickley's furniture with the exception of the hardware. Lacking satisfactory commercial hardware, Stickley hired metalsmiths to handcraft elongated strap hinges and forged drawer pulls (ill. 3). The resulting designs were indebted to the medieval-style hardware employed by British Arts and Crafts designers (vi). Otherwise, Stickley's metalwork reflected its construction techniques. Hammering and casting are traditional metalwork-forming methods. Because hammering epitomized the popular handcraft image, much of the period's metalwork was hammered, casting being reserved for unhammerable elements. The natural result of the hammering process is a circular organic form. Square forms and corners must be pieced and seamed, while a circular vessel can be hammered from one piece. Stickley's copper wall plaque (ill. 84), with its recessed center and naturalistic *repoussé* motifs, displays the organic esthetics common to much of the period's metalwork.[4]

The presence of hammermarks in Arts and Crafts metalwork signified hand-hammered construction, so objects were commonly left unplanished. Whereas, in preindustrial times, the skilled craftsman removed the marks of hand-hammering and planished the object to a smooth, bright finish (the challenge then being to craft the object as perfectly as possible), once a machine could produce a perfectly balanced, smooth and finished form, the craftsman felt obliged to leave the evidence of his hands. What once betrayed crude, imperfect craftsmanship now signified superior, handcrafted quality. A softer mat finish was favored by many of the period's metalworkers.

The more machine-made an object looked, of course, the less successful it was as an example of Arts and Crafts. While many, like Stickley, employed machines in the fabrication of objects, the finished product had to reflect the labor of hands. This is why Arts and Crafts objects are usually associated not with high-style, highly finished, preindustrial work, but with older, or more vernacular forms which were simply conceived and prominently featured the tell-tale signs of handcraftsmanship.

The one obvious exception to this is silver, where vernacular prototypes are rare. Especially in New England, Arts and Crafts silversmiths revived eighteenth-century forms, with more subdued hammermarks, and smoother finishes. The colonial revival was a contemporary phenomenon that had strong ties with the Arts and Crafts Movement. In 1899 the Boston Society of Arts and Crafts exhibited contemporary crafts alongside preindustrial pieces and encouraged their members to measure their work by the time-honored examples. Such practices, combined with Boston's patriotic traditions, encouraged silversmiths to imitate their forbears (viii).

Stickley was the most prominent champion of the American Arts and Crafts Movement, but many other craftsmen and manufacturers throughout the country shared in the

v   *Harvey Ellis (c.1885). Ellis joined*
Stickley's Workshops in 1903 and in less than
a year (he died in 1904) left an indelible mark
on the American Arts and Crafts Movement,
adding poetry and refinement to the honesty
and simplicity of Stickley's designs.
Courtesy of the Margaret Woodbury Strong
Museum, Rochester, N.Y.

Left

vi *The "Kelmscott" Cabinet, designed by
the British designer C. F. A. Voysey, executed
by F. Coote, and shown at the Arts and
Crafts Exhibition, 1899. With its strap
hinges and applied nameplates, the cabinet
exemplifies the decorative, neo-medieval
character of British Arts and Crafts furniture.
Courtesy The Fine Art Society, London.
Collection Cheltenham Art Gallery and
Museum*

Below

vii *Elbert Hubbard (c.1910). Hubbard's
Roycroft Shops, founded after he visited
William Morris's Kelmscott Press in 1894,
were to play a large part in popularizing Arts
and Crafts ideals throughout the United
States.
Courtesy Tod M. Volpe*

crusade. Elbert Hubbard (1856–1915) was equally zealous. Hubbard was the founder and entrepreneur behind the Roycroft Shops in East Aurora, New York. He visited William Morris and his Kelmscott Press in 1894 and, impressed with Morris's revival of the printing arts, returned to East Aurora and bought a small printing press.

Hubbard devoted himself to his new cause with evangelistic verve. He named his venture Roycroft for the seventeenth-century English bookbinding partners, Samuel and Thomas Roycroft. Soon, dissatisfied with commercial bookbinding, Hubbard established a bindery to service the press. A leather shop grew out of the bindery, and Hubbard's vision of a guild-like crafts community began to take shape. In addition to his own writings, he published exquisite art editions of works by other authors. Chamois and modeled leather bindings, imported handmade paper, special typefaces, and hand-illuminated initials characterized Roycroft books (ills. 121–4).

Furniture was produced at Roycroft as early as 1896, probably for the community's own use. By 1901 it was offered in the firm's mail-order catalogue. Like Stickley, Hubbard founded a metalworking shop to provide furniture hardware, and it also produced other utilitarian forms. Virtually all Roycroft products were prominently marked with the Roycroft name or the community's symbol, an orb and cross.[5]

Roycroft furniture is similar in conception to Stickley's Craftsman furniture, but more Gothic, a fact which reveals its British inspiration. As with most Arts and Crafts furniture, the emphasis on structure dictated an architectonic style that was simple and straightforward (ills. 29–31). The pervasive use of the Roycroft symbol or the Roycroft name in large Gothic-style letters lent a decorative effect which recalled more highly decorated English counterparts (vi). Like Stickley's Craftsman furniture, Roycroft furniture featured joined construction and quarter-sawn oak, though mahogany and ash were other options.

Roycroft metalwork bears the period's requisite hammer-marks. Roycroft designer Dard Hunter traveled to Vienna in 1908 where he visited the Wiener Werkstätte, the nucleus of the Austrian Arts and Crafts Movement.[6] Upon his return he introduced geometric motifs characteristic of the Werkstätte's preference for architectonic, linear forms, and quite different from the typical organic shapes of most American Arts and Crafts metalwork. The repetition of small squares seen in the Fern Dish and Bud Vase (ills. 89, 84) was Viennese-inspired. The same geometric character can be seen in the lamp (ill. 111) designed by Hunter.

The Roycroft Shops, like Stickley's Craftsman Workshops, offered lighting fixtures containing glass, but neither workshop produced glass. Of all crafts materials, glass was among the least accessible to single craftsmen or small studios. Even in preindustrial times, substantial capital was required to fund the construction of glass factories with their expensive furnaces. Consequently, most American Arts and Crafts glass was blown in large commercial studios, such as those run by Louis Comfort Tiffany or Frederick Carder, or assembled from plate glass obtained from one of the glass factories.[7] Roycroft craftsmen used imported glass for lighting fixtures and stained glass windows. The resulting designs reveal Dard Hunter's Viennese inspiration (ill. 112) as well as the influence of contemporary British design. The set of windows (ill. 113) is indebted not only to medieval stained glass, but also to the motifs of Charles Rennie Mackintosh.

The Roycroft Shops enjoyed national fame, largely through Roycroft publications and Hubbard's entrepreneurial supervision. Hubbard's dream of a successful crafts community was realized, but only briefly. He and his wife were drowned in the sinking of the *Lusitania* in 1915; their son Elbert (Bert) assumed leadership of the firm, but could not sustain it through the Depression, and in 1938 the Roycroft Shops were sold.

Whereas the Roycroft Shops were a distinctly profit-making enterprise, other Arts and Crafts communities had a more socialist orientation. The Byrdcliffe Colony in Woodstock, New York, was a craft community devoted to preserving preindustrial ideals. Hull House in Chicago was founded to relieve the penury of immigrants by teaching them skilled crafts and providing a place for them to practice. Craft shops and colonies arose around the country. Most were not as socialistic as Byrdcliffe, nor as capitalistic as Roycroft.[8] Societies of arts and crafts were also formed in many cities and communities, to patronize, exhibit, train, and facilitate the handicrafts. Participation in these shops and societies was by no means limited to professional craftsmen. The movement promoted the therapeutic benefits of handwork to amateurs. Lay participation was one of its most vital aspects.

The most eccentric furniture of the American Arts and Crafts Movement was made by a former playwright and actor, Charles Rohlfs (1853–1936) of Buffalo, New York. Rohlfs established a shop in Buffalo in 1890 and specialized in domestic furniture, office suites, and custom work. Even at the height of his production, he employed no more than eight assistants. Despite the size of his shop, Rohlfs achieved international recognition through his submissions to the Exhibition of Modern Decorative Arts in Turin in 1902.

Stylistically, Rohlfs's highly individual designs have more in common with the German interpretation of Art Nouveau, known as Jugendstil, than with the light, elegant lines of French Art Nouveau. His forms are dynamic and highly carved, with curving, life-like shapes and emphatic sinuous carved decoration which constrasts markedly with Stickley's geometric conceptions. Rohlfs's son recounts that his father's billowing pipe smoke provided inspiration for some of the carved designs.[9] In contrast with Art Nouveau furniture, however, Rohlfs rarely sculpted in three-dimensional shapes but constructed his furniture from planes of wood that were shaped or relieved by carving. This planar design, and Rohlfs's preference for oak and for mortice and tenon joinery relate his works to Stickley, Roycroft, and other Arts and Crafts furniture.

Rohlfs is another instance of an Arts and Crafts designer looking to vernacular prototypes for source material. The chalet desk (ill. 13) has Gothic-arch shaped sides, but the shape of the desk and its heavy carving relate to northern European folk traditions. Non-Western inspiration seems likely in the pierced slab sides of the rocking chair (ill. 20). The circular carved design may have been inspired by the Chinese character for longevity, *shou*, which was commonly used as a circular decorative motif on Chinese ceramics and textiles in the Ming and Qing dynasties.

Oriental and Art Nouveau influences were also visible in the works of the Prairie School. Their houses – long, low, earth-hugging residences – were fashioned of natural materials, and unified in design from interiors to landscape. Dedicated to the Arts and Crafts concept of harmonious domestic design, the designers of this school treated decorative arts as well as architecture.

The most inventive designer to use Art Nouveau elements was Louis Sullivan (1856–1924), who is often considered to be the father of the Prairie School, though he is himself better known for commercial than domestic buildings. Sullivan established his Chicago practice in partnership with Dankmar Adler in 1875. Rejecting Art Nouveau's meandering asymmetrical nature, he imposed symmetry and control on highly organic, active designs. The result was tight, dynamic, and distinctive, as seen in the elevator grille for the Chicago Stock Exchange (ill. 93).

The same tight control and interplay of geometry and naturalism can be seen in the Babson house commissions (ill. 127). Sullivan's chief draftsman, George Grant Elmslie (1871–1952) assisted him with the Babson house before he left Sullivan in 1909 to team up with William Purcell and George Feick. The new firm's prowess with increasingly rectilinear design is evidenced in Elmslie's 1912 clock (ill. 32) and the spindle-sided cube chairs designed for the Merchant's Bank in Winona, Minnesota in 1911 (ill. 34).

Another of Sullivan's protégés, George Washington Maher (1864–1926), established his own practice in 1888. A Prairie School advocate of unified design, Maher characteristically designed a special motif for each commission, and repeated it throughout interior and exterior spaces. Maher called his concept the "motif rhythm theory" and attributed his inspiration for the motifs to "the necessity of the situation and local color and conditions."[10] The armchair illustrated here (ill. 35) was designed in 1912 for Rockledge, a summer residence in Minnesota. Its arched crest rail defined by horizontal flanges was a motif repeated throughout the house, as were the pyramidal shapes of the canted stiles, and the trapezoidal guttae decorating the capitals of the columns.[11]

The seminal figure of the Prairie School was also a student of Louis Sullivan, Frank Lloyd Wright (1867–1959).

Wright set up his own practice in Chicago in 1893 and was a founding member of the Chicago Arts and Crafts Society in 1897. Wright's designs from this period exemplify the Arts and Crafts principles of simple style, natural materials, and integrated design. He conceived of decorative arts as interior architecture, forms which contributed to a unified design scheme:

The "grammar" of the house, is its manifest articulation of all its parts – the "speech" it uses . . . . Everything has a related articulation in relation to the whole and all belongs together because all are speaking the same language.[12]

Wright's strict insistence on a unified environment may have developed from his admiration for Japanese art and culture, where all components contribute to a total esthetic. Also in common with Japanese precepts were his respect for natural materials and use of cantilevered construction.

Of all the Prairie School architects, Wright was the most geometric in his approach. His designs for furniture, glass, and metalwork are boldly conceived of planes, spindles, cubes, circles, and triangles (ills. 23, 92). Still, the organic theme of the Arts and Crafts Movement pervades his work. His geometric constructions are abstractions from local flora or landscape. The long low lines of his Chicago residences echoed the Illinois prairie. In the Dana house doors, for example, Wright used an abstraction of the sumac leaf (ill. 107). Organic design sources were central to his philosophy.

In contrast with Stickley and other Eastern Arts and Crafts designers, Wright and the Prairie School architects placed more importance on the unified environment than on construction and handcraftsmanship. At the Craftsman or Roycroft shops, the paramount design factor was the object's construction and handcrafted appearance. Stickley and Hubbard catered to a middle-class clientele and encouraged harmonious design through the use of simply designed, handcrafted home furnishings. Wright and his colleagues were designing for a higher socioeconomic level which could afford their stricter standards for unity.

Wright's furniture design is accordingly uninterrupted by paneled construction, protruding mortices and keys, or visible pegs and pins. Whereas most Arts and Crafts designers discreetly admitted machinery where it speeded the process without compromising quality, Wright openly embraced it, adapting his designs in order to exploit the machine's capabilities (ills. 22–28).

Wright's views on machinery were not accepted by most Arts and Crafts philosophers who believed first and foremost in the craftsman. The Chicago Arts and Crafts Society considered the machine acceptable "in so far as it relieves the workman from drudgery . . . ,"[13] but pledged itself to the promotion of handcraft. Chicago's finest silversmiths in this period were just such craftsmen. In their progressive designs, they contrasted with New England Arts and Crafts silversmiths who relied heavily on colonial prototypes.

Among the earliest and most prominent of Chicago metalworking enterprises was the Kalo Shops, founded in 1900 by design school graduate Clara Barck (1868–1965). The name was taken from the Greek word *kalos*, meaning beautiful. The Kalo Shops began as an all-female venture producing weaving and leather goods, but after Barck's marriage to an amateur metalsmith, George Welles, in 1905, the focus turned to silver. At its height, Kalo employed twenty-five silversmiths, producing simple, rounded, hand-hammered forms exemplifying the Kalo motto, "Beautiful, useful, and enduring." The early sugar and cream set and the tray (ills. 100, 101) are both inlaid with semiprecious stones in the contemporary British style (ix). The silver pitcher by Lebolt & Company illustrates the influence of Kalo and related crafts concerns on the Midwestern market. Lebolt was an established jewelry store that added a hand-wrought silver workshop in 1912. Lebolt silver ranged from elaborate Art Nouveau *repoussé* designs to simple Kalo-inspired forms, as seen in illustration 101.

Another prominent Chicago metalsmith, Robert Jarvie (1865–1941), was famous for candlesticks and presentation trophies, in base metals as well as silver. A self-trained amateur, Jarvie began producing brass, copper, or bronze candlesticks in simple, fluid designs (ill. 97) around 1900. He opened the Jarvie Shop in 1904, and expanded his repertoire to include a variety of domestic forms, adding pewter to his usual materials. He made silver trophies as special commissions, and his innovative designs were so successful that after 1910 he specialized in this area.

California, too, produced its own group of Arts and Crafts designers. Around 1900, Shreve & Company of San Francisco, a highly mechanized and well-established firm, introduced hand-wrought Arts and Crafts patterns. In flatware and hollow-ware, the strapwork designs were characteristically medieval in inspiration (ill. 96). Dutch-born Dirk Van Erp (1859–1933) must be considered the superlative Western artisan in base metals. Van Erp was a naval coppersmith at the Mare Island Shipyards in 1900. His hobby of making vases from discarded shell casings became a full-time business in 1908. Van Erp emphasized the hammering process in his simple circular designs. He oxidized his pieces with various patinas to achieve color variations from nutty brown to red, and paired the richly toned lamp bases with luminous mica shades (ills. 87, 116–17).

Van Erp's success was linked to the prosperity of the arts community in San Francisco, which included architect Bernard Maybeck and artist-craftsmen Arthur and Lucia Mathews. Arthur Mathews (1860–1945) was a French-trained American painter and university professor who married his student, Lucia Kleinhans (1870–1955). They established The Furniture Shop in 1906 to supply specially designed interiors to San Franciscans rebuilding after the earthquake. The shop employed numerous craftsmen to produce their highly decorated and colorful products, ranging from murals to furnishings. The ornamental appearance of the Mathews's works contrasts greatly with New York and Chicago arts and crafts, but, in common with the movement, the Mathews emphasized craft and integrated design schemes (ill. 38). Their work is the strongest link with the decorative neo-medieval furniture of the British Arts and Crafts Movement, by such designers as Edward Burne-Jones, Philip Webb, and William Morris (x, xi). Their allegorical style and bright colors are attributable to Arthur Mathews's Beaux-Arts training and his admiration of Japanese art, popular during his time in Paris.

The most significant Arts and Crafts designers in California were the architect brothers Greene and Greene. Charles Sumner Greene (1868–1957) and Henry Mather Greene (1870–1954) were born in Ohio and educated at the Arts and Crafts Movement-inspired Manual Training School in St. Louis, Missouri. After graduating from the architecture program at the Massachusetts Institute of Technology, the brothers traveled to California to visit their parents, recently retired to the fashionable resort community of Pasadena. En route to California, the Greenes attended the World's Columbian Exposition in Chicago where they were deeply impressed by the Japanese temple on display. Already sensitive to the craftsman principles of natural materials and honest construction, they were drawn to the exposed joinery and timber construction of Japanese architecture. They subsequently studied and collected examples of Oriental art.

Finding California congenial, the Greenes established a practice in Pasadena. Like other Arts and Crafts architects, they preferred to design total environments, including interior furnishings and landscapes. The humble bungalow, recommended by Stickley in *The Craftsman* as the ideal middle-class Arts and Crafts home, was already quite popular in California, and, for Pasadena's most affluent residents, the Greenes designed the ultimate bungalows of the period. With their rustic shingles, healthful sleeping porches and low, overhanging eaves derived from Oriental examples, they fitted into the California landscape as Prairie School designs had harmonized with the Illinois prairie.

The Greenes' esthetic was more decorative than Wright's, and more stylized than Stickley's. Like Stickley, they emphasized construction details as a form of decoration. Visible pegs, keys, and tenons are common, and sometimes serve no function other than decoration. The distinguishing factor in the Greenes' esthetic was their adaptation of Oriental concepts and motifs. They softened stark structural elements with rounded corners, subtly curved transitions, and abstract inlaid motifs or applied carving (ills. 36, 37). The results are the most eloquent of all American Arts and Crafts furniture. After touring America and visiting Charles Greene, British Arts and Crafts designer C. R. Ashbee wrote in 1909: "Like [Frank] Lloyd Wright the spell of Japan is on him. He feels the beauty and makes magic out of the horizontal line, but there is in his work more tenderness, more subtlety, more self-effacement than in Wright's work...."[14]

Right

viii   *Silver water pitcher by Arthur Stone, Gardner, Massachusetts, early 20th Century, exemplifying the prevalence of colonial designs in American Arts and Crafts silver. Courtesy Robert W. Skinner Inc., Boston/ Bolton, Massachusetts*

Below

ix   *Silver designs by C. R. Ashbee (1863– 1942), a leader of the British Arts and Crafts Movement. The use of semiprecious stones, characteristic of British Arts and Crafts silver, influenced such American pieces as the Kalo Shops sugar and cream set (ill. 100). Courtesy of Christie's, London*

Oriental as well as European influences were fundamental to the development of American Arts and Crafts ceramics, the most popular medium of the movement. Ceramics was an approachable craft to the novice, and had a special appeal for many women who already practiced the Victorian hobby of china painting. Socially banned from practicing many crafts, women turned to ceramics (xii). Interest was further awakened by national and international expositions. Foreign exhibits also challenged American potters to refine their skills. Art pottery was often a relatively inexpensive way for the American consumer to acquire art for the home and an avid market grew, supplied by a burgeoning number of potteries, until the Depression dampened the economy.

Stylistically, most American art pottery falls into two groups: wares emphasizing form and glaze, and those emphasizing applied, or manipulated, decoration. Exhibits of Oriental, Oriental-inspired French, and realistic-style French wares at the 1876 Centennial Exposition in Philadelphia inspired many of the earliest American art potters to strive for effects that resulted in these two approaches.

Among them was Hugh C. Robertson (1844–1908) of the Chelsea Keramic Art Works in Boston. After visiting the Exposition in Philadelphia, Robertson devoted himself to glaze experimentation. He continued his experiments as manager of the Dedham factory, producing numerous vases such as the example in illustration 68. Theophilus Brouwer, Jr. (1864–1932), of Middle Lane Pottery on Long Island, was a self-taught potter who devised a glaze technique he called fire painting. Brouwer used luster glazes, reduction firing,[15] and gold leaf to achieve the unique effects shown in illustration 67. Little is known about Cornelius Brauckman, who founded the Grand Feu pottery in Los Angeles in 1912. *Grand feu* or high-fired wares required technical skill, and the pottery was distinguished by the extraordinary glazes achieved at higher temperatures (ill. 69).

The most successful and influential glaze innovation was the work of William H. Grueby (1867-1925), founder of Boston's Grueby Faience Company in 1894. Grueby was inspired by French exhibits at the 1893 World's Columbian Exposition in Chicago. By 1897 he had perfected his now-famous "cucumber" glaze, a thick, mat, rind-like green (ills. 53, 54). A 1904 Grueby brochure described it: "This peculiar texture can be compared to the smooth surface of a melon or the bloom of a leaf, avoiding the extreme brilliancy of high glazes as well as the dull monotony of the mat finish."[16] In keeping with the vegetal characteristics of the glaze, Grueby's chief designer George Kendrick devised organic, plant-like vases, bowls, and lamp bases that were hand-made by women art students.

The only Eastern pottery to rival Grueby's market success was the Fulper Pottery in Flemington, New Jersey. Already a commercial pottery, Fulper introduced their art line, called Vase-Kraft, in 1910. The simple, classical Vase-Kraft shapes served as vehicles for superb glazes in mat, crystalline, and flambé finishes (ills. 57, 58).

The maverick of forms and glazes was an extremely talented potter in Biloxi, Mississippi, George E. Ohr (1857–1918). Ohr used a potter's wheel to "throw" extremely fine, eggshell-thin forms which he then crumpled and twisted into unprecedented and contorted shapes. His glazes were equally eccentric, in bright colors, metallic lusters, and blistered textures (ills. 77–79). Ohr's works were ahead of their time, and presage the expressionistic forms and glazes of American studio ceramics.

Influences from European Art Nouveau occasionally overlapped with the American Arts and Crafts Movement, as did those from the colonial revival. Art Nouveau was also promoted as a reform style, rejecting high Victorian eclecticism in favor of natural, organic forms. In Ohio, the French ceramist Jacques Sicard (1865–1923) gave his name to a line of special art wares at the Weller factory in Zanesville. Produced from 1902 to 1912, Sicardo wares were distinguished by rich metallic luster glazes on molded floral forms of Art Nouveau inspiration (ill. 66). In New York, Louis Comfort Tiffany produced a line of art pottery known as *favrile*, meaning hand-made. Tiffany also favored molded organic designs whose forms and glazes imitated nature (ills. 61, 62). Similar effects were achieved by Artus Van Briggle, who established his own pottery in Colorado Springs in 1901. Van Briggle, formerly of the Rookwood Pottery in Cincinnati, had spent three years studying in Paris. His lyrical, sculptural designs were not imitative of nature, like Tiffany's, but were derivative and abstract (ills. 48–50).

Although less Art Nouveau in style, William Gates's Gates Potteries in Chicago also emphasized molded forms and special glazes. First offered in 1902, his Teco line of art pottery consisted of stylized organic designs (ill. 65) as well as more architectonic, geometric forms (ill. 64). Gates's response to Grueby green was lighter and bluer, a soft sea color that outsold the company's other colors.

The second group of American art potteries focused on applied or manipulated decoration, though form and glaze were also important. The founder of this tradition was Mary Louise McLaughlin (1847–1939) from Cincinnati, who was also inspired by French ceramics at the Centennial Exposition. McLaughlin set out to copy the Limoges art wares with their extensive underglaze slip decoration.[17] Her successful results became known as Cincinnati Limoges. Maria Longworth Nichols (1849–1932), a fellow ceramist, had recently founded the Rookwood Pottery in 1880 (xii). She employed and perfected McLaughlin's methods with great commercial success. The brown palette of Rookwood standard ware (ills. 42, 43) was copied by numerous potteries.

Rookwood hired professional decorators and chemists who devised new techniques of pictorial decoration. The high glaze Sea Green (ill. 45) was introduced in 1894, followed by the highly successful Vellum glaze in 1904 (xiii). The latter was a breakthrough in glaze chemistry, a translucent mat glaze permitting underglaze decoration.

Women decorators working at the
Rookwood Pottery c.1890, approximately ten
years after the Cincinnati pottery was
founded by Maria Longworth Nichols.
Courtesy Cincinnati Historical Society

One of the strengths of the art pottery movement in America was its adaptability to differing scales of operations. Award-winning exposition entries might originate from one-potter studios, academic classrooms, local potteries, and large commercial enterprises. Overbeck was a small, localized pottery in Cambridge City, Indiana. Founded in 1911 by four sisters, Overbeck deserves notice for a style quite distinctive from the widespread Rookwood influence. Overbeck wares are recognizable by their specially developed glaze colors: mat and glossy shades of grape, hyacinth blue, turquoise, yellow, raspberry, and green, as well as earthier hues. The sisters specialized in glaze inlay and carved decoration (ill. 83).

Newcomb Pottery was the most successful Southern art pottery. It was administered by the all-female Newcomb College in New Orleans with the intention of training young women in skills which would allow them to pursue an acceptable career. Newcomb taught design, decoration, and glazing. Professional potters were hired to throw the pots, as wheelwork was considered too arduous for women. Design instructor Mary Sheerer (1865–1954) explained the pottery's philosophy: "The whole thing was to be a southern product, made of southern clays, by southern artists, decorated with southern subjects."[18] Thus Newcomb wares feature Southern flora or fauna, in a distinctive palette of blues and greens. Their high-glazed wares (ill. 51) were complemented by a mat glaze after 1910, influenced by Rookwood's example (ill. 52).

One of the outstanding potters of the period was Adelaide Alsop Robineau (1865–1929) of Syracuse, New York. An avid china painter, Mrs. Robineau studied with Charles Binns[19] at Alfred University in New York State and began experimenting with the most challenging of ceramic bodies, porcelain. Her husband assisted her with firings and glaze development. Robineau laboriously carved or pierced her pieces, often reworking a piece through several firings. Her spectacular results reveal Art Nouveau influences (ills. 73, 74) and Chinese inspiration (ill. 71).

When Edward Lewis set out to found a state-of-the-art pottery in University City, Missouri, in 1910, he courted the Robineaus to move from Syracuse. His brilliant staff also included the French ceramic genius Taxile Doat (1851–1938),[20] and the influential English ceramist Frederick H. Rhead (1880–1942).[21] Conceived as part of a broader women's education scheme, University City lasted only five years, but in that short period produced exquisite art porcelain with carved decoration (ill. 75) or exotic glazes (ill. 70). University City won the Grand Prize at the International Exposition of Decorative Arts at Turin in 1911, despite intense European competition. The superlative piece was the Scarab Vase (ill. 71), made by Mrs. Robineau while in Missouri.

World War I sounded the death knell for many Arts and Crafts pursuits. Wartime realities intruded on America's nostalgic preoccupation with the craftsman lifestyle. Many craftsmen continued successful businesses after the war, but the Depression effectively drained the movement's vitality. Its legacy was more enduring, however, and survives in our attitudes about domestic environments, craft as art, and the artistic value of decorative arts in general. As a result of the Arts and Crafts Movement, art enjoys broader definition in our society, and a broader spectrum of society enjoys art.

Furniture

The furniture designed by the American Arts and Crafts Movement cabinetmakers and architects was characterized by simplicity and cleanliness of form, honesty of construction, attention to detail, and a love of material naturally expressed. Durability was emphasized; each piece was made to be used and made to last. The value of handcraftsmanship was especially stressed. Mortices and tenons, and doweling, replaced the nail and screw. Superfluous ornament was assiduously avoided; an object's structural elements became its main source of decoration. Gustav Stickley's publication *The Craftsman* exemplified this doctrine, and Frank Lloyd Wright carried it to its logical conclusion in his use of the machine to eliminate the most rudimentary labor-intensive stages of furniture production. Form, proportion, line, and overall design became part of the modern furniture-maker's vocabulary.

Craftsman Workshops: Gustav Stickley, Harvey Ellis

The poppy tea table (1) designed by Gustav Stickley (1857–1942) and executed at his Craftsman Workshops in Eastwood, New York, around 1900, is representative of his early experiments and was clearly inspired by the British Arts and Crafts Movement and continental Art Nouveau examples he saw during his trips to Europe in the late 1890s. The model is referred to in an article in the October 1900 issue of *House Beautiful* as inspired by natural forms in which the stem, leaf, and flowers have been incorporated into the construction. "This is noticeable in some of the tables, where the legs suggest the stem of the plant, while the tops reproduce the lines of the open flower. This idea is quaintly demonstrated in the Poppy tables..."[1] Two months later in *House Beautiful* the same model was illustrated, described now as a "Celandine Tea Table" model No. 327, finished in gun-metal green and priced at $6.

Further information on the table has been provided by John Crosby Freeman in *The Forgotten Rebel* (1966), in which he quotes Stickley on the motivation behind these early organic designs and the reason why he abandoned them:

In 1900 I stopped using the standard patterns and finishes, and began to make all kinds of furniture after my own designs, independently of what other people were doing.... My frequent trips to Europe ... interested me much in the decorative use of plant forms, and I followed the suggestion.... After experimenting with a number of pieces, such as small tables giving in their form a conventionalized suggestion of such plant forms as the mallow, the sunflower, and the pansy, I abandoned the idea. Conventionalized plant forms are beautiful and fitting when used solely for decoration, but anyone who starts to make a piece of furniture with a decorative form in mind, starts at the wrong end. The sole consideration at the basis of the design must be the thing itself and not its ornamentation.[2]

1 Poppy Tea Table, designed by Gustav
Stickley, Craftsman Workshops (c.1900).
American white oak, quarter sawn. A
quatrefoil top, designed as an open flower,
with incised linear detailing. The table is
raised on plant form flat legs with heart-
shaped motifs with pierced centers below the
top, the lower overlapping stretchers pinned
in the center and fastened with tenon-and-key
construction. 24in. (61cm.) high; 20in.
(50.8cm.) diameter.
Collection of David and Beth Cathers

2 Library Table, designed by Gustav
Stickley, Craftsman Workshops (1901–09).
Oak and leather. The hexagonal top has a
studded leather surface above 6 rectangular
legs linked by arched aprons. The stretchers
are attached by tenon-and-key construction
and pinned in the center by a vertical faceted
dowel. 30½in. (77.5cm.) high; 48½in.
(123.2cm.) diameter.
Private Collection

Although Stickley dropped the Art Nouveau form of this tea table from his repertoire within a short time, he retained two of its structural elements: the use of the chamfered cleat by which the table top was braced on its underside to prevent warping, and the incorporation of the overlapping stretchers pinned in the center. This form anticipated some of the more powerful and distinctive stretchers found in later examples of his furniture, such as the library table (2) which first appeared in his 1901 catalogue and was offered virtually unchanged for the next eight years. It was produced with a plain wood or leather top.

With its emphasis on massive proportions, strength, and durability, this design precisely represents Stickley's philosophy of furniture-making. Important modifications were introduced in 1909, particularly the removal of the tenon-and-key construction by which the stretchers were attached to the legs; the arched aprons were straightened; the legs became square rather than rectangular; and the original three stretchers were replaced by six half-stretchers joined in the center.[3]

In about 1902 Stickley produced a double bookcase (3) which is extremely rare, if not unique. A similar model appears in a line drawing in Stickley's periodical *The Craftsman* in November 1902, in which tenons are visible on the top and bottom of the front legs. In addition, both pairs of doors and cupboards are recessed, unlike this example. The lower pair of cupboards, which are not found in other Stickley models, suggest that this was a special commission or a prototype which was not put into regular production. In his early years Stickley experimented with many different forms, so it is possible that this piece was considered impractical for mass production, perhaps because of its expense.

The method of construction indicates that this bookcase belongs to Stickley's first "Mission" period (1900–04). The back is made of vertical chamfered boards, a technique requiring more labor and materials than the paneled backs of later models.

During this early period, Stickley produced a bench settle with slightly concave armrests (4), which is characteristic of his work in its monumentality, lack of carved ornamentation, and severe contours. The latter are somewhat softened in this model by the undulating flow of the armrests into the foot, but it is still essentially a functional piece of furniture.

Also typical of this period is a reclining chair in oak (5) that was designed for reading. Other notable Morris chairs by Stickley incorporated slat and spindle sides, which, from a design point of view, are usually more successful. Though this model has open sides, which in normal circumstances allowed very little creativity, its arched armrests impart movement and comfort. The gentle curve is repeated on the aprons to create unity. The horizontal side slats, used for reinforcement, were eliminated from later models.

The Morris chair took its name from a widely acclaimed reclining chair introduced by Morris & Company in London in 1866. A staple of Aesthetic Movement interiors of the 1880s and 1890s, the model became a symbol of the Arts and Crafts Movement in the U.S.A. In all, Stickley designed seven Morris chairs, the first of which he patented in October, 1901. He described his largest model, to be located in the library or in the living room near the

3 *Double Bookcase, designed by Gustav Stickley, Craftsman Workshops (c.1902). Oak, quarter sawn, and handwrought copper. The piece has an openwork gallery above twin bookcases, each with a pair of doors, with 12 glass panels and copper bail handles mounted on rectangular plates, opening to shelf space; the lower pair of cupboard doors is set with strap hinges and matching bail handles and escutcheons. 69½in. (176.5cm.) high; 60in. (152.4cm.) wide; 13¾in. (34.4cm.) deep. Collection of David and Beth Cathers*

Opposite

4   Bench Settle, designed by Gustav
Stickley, Craftsman Workshops (c.1902).
Oak, quarter sawn. The back is made of 11
planks bordered by flaring supports which
continue to recessed armrests and outcurved
feet. 56in. (142.2cm.) high; 71in. (180.3cm.)
wide.
Private Collection

Below

5   Reclining Chair, designed by Gustav
Stickley, Craftsman Workshops (c.1902).
Black stained oak. The back is adjustable and
has 4 curved horizontal splats; the gently
arched arms are secured to the front legs by
extending tenons, the 4 legs braced on the
exterior with curved corbels above a side splat
and arched apron. 38¾in (98.4cm.)
maximum height; 31in. (78.8cm.) wide; 37in.
(94cm.) deep.
Collection of Mr. and Mrs. John M. Angelo

6 *Fall-front Desk, designed by Harvey Ellis for Gustav Stickley, Craftsman Workshops (1903–04).*
American white oak, quarter sawn. The paneled fall front is inlaid in pewter, copper, and exotic woods and opens to a fitted interior with octagonal inkwells and an oval pen tray.
46½in. (118.1cm.) high; 42in. (106.7cm.) wide; 11½in. (29.2cm.) deep.
Collection of the Virginia Museum of Fine Arts, Richmond, Virginia. Gift of Sydney and Frances Lewis

hearth, as "a big, deep chair that means comfort to a tired man when he comes home after the day's work." It was seldom that Stickley's two brothers, Leopold and John George, were able to make improvements to their older brother's designs, but a Morris chair introduced by them around 1910 successfully eliminated the side slat and also increased the decorative appeal of the chair by extending the corbels downwards.

By 1903 Harvey Ellis (1852–1904) had joined the Craftsman Workshops, and one of the first pieces on which he collaborated was a fall-front desk in American white oak (6). It appears that the basic form had been determined by Stickley before Ellis's arrival, but Ellis introduced refinements that lightened its visual heaviness. This was achieved primarily through the introduction of the three inlaid plant motifs. Stickley discussed the technique in an article in the January 1904 issue of *The Craftsman*, noting that the decoration was to "make interesting what otherwise would have been a too large area of plain, flat surface. It, in every case, emphasizes the structural lines, accenting in most instances the vertical elements, and so giving a certain slenderness of effect to a whole which were otherwise too solid and heavy."[4]

Further refinements introduced by Ellis to this desk included the elimination of the tenon-and-key joints in Stickley's earlier model, and the introduction of an arched apron beneath the open shelf, serving both to strengthen the structure and to give it grace and lightness. Ellis's attention to detail is evident in the placement of the desk's central drawer, which is set back slightly from its front. This allows it to correspond to the recessed panels in the upper cupboard doors and fall-front, helping further to unify the composition.

Ellis left an indelible mark on the American Arts and Crafts Movement during his fleeting stay at the Craftsman Workshops (April 1903–January 1904). Born in Rochester, New York, his later peripatetic and dissolute lifestyle was soon manifest in his uncompleted schooling, followed by his dismissal from West Point in 1871, a secret marriage to an actress (annuled by his father), and several other short-lived ventures. After a trip to Europe, he returned to Rochester, where he made the acquaintance of Henry H. Richardson, at that time one of America's most influential architects. This had a far-reaching effect on Ellis, and in 1879, in partnership with his brother Charles, he opened an architectural office in Rochester. A stint as a journeyman architect followed in St. Paul and other Midwestern cities between 1886 and 1889. His activities during those years are hard to unravel as he often worked under a pseudonym.

By 1894 he was back in Rochester as a result of his father's death. Tiring of architecture, he concentrated his talents increasingly on painting and drawing, while becoming attracted to the works of the Arts and Crafts Movement. After separating from his wife in 1901, he accepted an offer from Stickley, in April 1903, to work as an illustrator for *The Craftsman*. He soon became involved in furniture design, particularly in renderings of ornamental inlays. However, the combination of alcohol and self-neglect led to his premature death, in poverty and obscurity, at the age of fifty-two.

Ellis's impact on Stickley's furniture was profound. He brought a refined and poetic quality to models which might have become increasingly monumental and severe in Stickley's pursuit of honesty and simplicity. Ellis's soft touch, evident across the entire gamut of his designs for textiles, graphics, architecture, and furniture, showed his full grasp of contemporary developments in Glasgow, London, and Vienna. The architect-designer Claude Bragdon paid an elegant tribute to his old friend in 1908: "Harvey Ellis was a genius. Had it not been for the evil fairy which presided at his birth and ruled his destiny, Harvey Ellis ... might have been a prominent, instead of obscure, figure in [the] esthetic awakening of America."[5] Today his work is seen to have injected a breath of fresh air and levity into the uniform, and sometimes ponderous, world of Stickley interiors.

Harvey Ellis's hallmarks can be seen on four additional pieces that were produced between 1903 and 1910 (7, 8, 9, 10). The two-door bookcase shows his influence in the arched apron, the overhanging top, the absence of hardware, and the paneled back. The sides, however, are assembled with exposed tenons, which are typical of Stickley's designs rather than Ellis's; the model may therefore have been a joint effort. On the other hand, the classical device of a pilaster on each side of the doors is more typical of Ellis than of Stickley.

The arched apron appears again in Ellis's armchair (9), as well as the inlaid ornamentation on the central back splat. Several influences are evident in Ellis's furniture inlays, the most common of which are the attenuated, conventionalized floral and plant motifs, such as the one used in his side chair for Stickley (8). His designs often recall similar inlaid ornamentation by M. H. Baillie Scott and members of the London Guild of Handicraft. Occasionally Ellis would borrow also from Japanese or American Indian designs. Stickley had previously been opposed to the use of applied ornament on furniture, but Ellis somehow managed to exert artistic freedom on this issue, with the result that Stickley later abruptly reversed his former opinion. In his posthumous tribute to Ellis in *The Craftsman* (January 1904) he wrote,

This ornament, like that of the Greeks, appears to proceed from within outward. It bears no trace of having been applied. It consists of fine markings, discs, and other figures of pewter and copper, which, like stems of plants and obscured, simplified floral forms, seem to pierce the surface of the wood beneath ... in the ornament of the cabinet-work, the silvery lines with their expanded terminals of bright bronze or colored woods, contrast well with the gray-brown of the oak.[6]

Ellis's dresser in gray maple (10) can be identified as his creation by the gently bowed legs, the arched apron, and the overhanging top shelves – all of which he introduced during his nine-months stay at Eastwood, and which Stickley retained after Ellis's death.

The dresser provides a rare example of a Stickley furniture design made in a wood other than American white oak. Sharing his preference with most Arts and Crafts cabinetmakers, Stickley wrote,

Oak is to Craftsman furniture what mahogany was to the French, English, and Colonial furniture of the eighteenth century – a wood perfectly adapted to the use made of it – and in addition to this, it has a natural quality which I can best express by the term "friendly," that is, a certain strength of fiber and grain and a mellowness of color and surface which seems to offer itself to everyday use and wear.[7]

7 *Two-door Bookcase, inspired by Harvey Ellis, Craftsman Workshops (1906–10). Oak, quarter sawn. Each door has a pair of glazed upper square panels and lower panels divided by a central splat. The doors, which have flanking pilasters, open to 3 adjustable shelves. The lower arched apron is matched by cut-outs on the sides. 57¹³⁄₁₆in. (145.3cm.) high; 42½in. (108cm.) wide; 14⅛in. (35.9cm.) deep. Collection of Darrel Couturier; photo York Photographic Design, Los Angeles, California*

Below left

8 Side Chair, designed by Harvey Ellis for Gustav Stickley, Craftsman Workshops (1903–04).
American white oak and rush. The central splat is inlaid in pewter, copper, and exotic stained woods. The square caned seat is raised on 4 gently bowed square legs linked in the front by an upper arched stretcher and on the sides and back by further stretchers. 47½in. (120.6cm.) high; 18½in. (47cm.) wide; 17in. (43.2cm.) deep.
Collection of David and Beth Cathers

Below right

9 Armchair, designed by Harvey Ellis for Gustav Stickley, Craftsman Workshops (1903–04).
Oak, rush, pewter, and wood inlays. The broad central splat is inlaid in pewter and pale wood veneers with an elongated Arts and Crafts motif. 47in. (119.4cm.) high.
Collection of the Carnegie Museum of Art, Pittsburgh, Pennsylvania. Decorative Arts Purchase Fund: Gift of Mr. and Mrs. Aleon Deitch, by exchange, 1982

Opposite

10 Dresser, designed by Harvey Ellis for Gustav Stickley, Craftsman Workshops (1904–10).
Gray maple, pewter, and wood inlays. The upper section has 2 compartments centering on 3 short drawers above a broad rectangular shelf. Beneath are 3 graduating drawers. The spherical drawer pulls are within circular recessed pewter and exotic inlaid wood pull-plates. 43in. (109.2cm.) high; 42in. (106.7cm.) wide; 20in. (50.8cm.) deep.
Private Collection

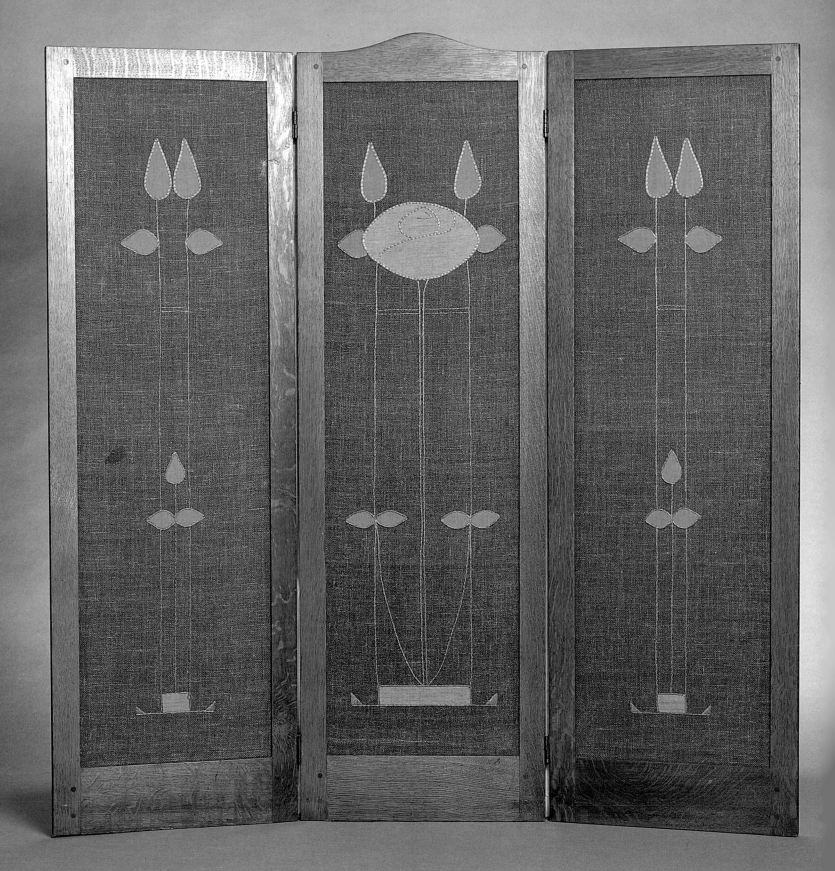

11   *Three-fold Screen, designed by Gustav
Stickley, Craftsman Workshops (c.1904).
Oak, "Craftsman Canvas," and leather.
Mounted in "Craftsman Canvas" decorated
with appliquéd linen floral motifs. 59¼in.
(150.5cm.) height of the central panel;
57⅞in. (147cm.) height of the flanking
panels; 18½in. (47cm.) width of individual
panels.
Collection of James and Janeen Marrin*

12   *Spindle-back Settee, designed by Gustav
Stickley, Craftsman Workshops (1905–07).
Oak and rush. The row of vertical spindles at
the back is matched on the sides by bands of
spindles extending to the lower side stretchers.
48½in. (123cm.) high; 47½in. (120cm.)
wide; 25in. (63.5cm.) deep.
Collection of David and Beth Cathers*

The Craftsman Workshops continued in business for more than ten years after Ellis's death, and during those years Stickley produced many objects of originality and beauty. Around 1904 he introduced a three-fold screen (11) mounted in a material resembling burlap which Stickley called "Craftsman Canvas." It was described in one of the firm's catalogues as "One of the most satisfying of our materials for portières, pillow covers, upholstery – in fact, for any use where a rugged effected is desired."[8]

The February 1905 issue of *The Craftsman* included two versions of the three-fold screen, both decorated with formalized roses in a style derivative of Charles Rennie Mackintosh and the Vienna Secession. In fact, Stickley appears to have borrowed the Scottish rose without any attempt to disguise its origin.

On 8 August 1905, Stickley patented a line of spindle furniture (12) and examples were illustrated in *The Craftsman* from September 1905 for roughly the next eighteen months.[9] Perhaps influenced by the delicacy of Ellis's designs, Stickley's introduction of the light spindle in place of the heavy Mission splat represented a new departure.

Although there is no surviving documentation to link Stickley's spindle-back settee to either Frank Lloyd Wright or Charles Rennie Mackintosh, their influence is evident in the appearance of height which the spindles achieve. Both the spindle furniture designed by Wright for his Prairie houses and the ladder-back models by Mackintosh were familiar to Stickley, and one reason for introducing the spindle line may have been his knowledge that Wright's clients were invariably enthusiastic about this style. Stickley may also have been reacting to Wright's criticism that Mission furniture was clumsy and therefore unsuitable for the houses he designed.

Charles Rohlfs

Charles Rohlfs (1853–1936), the son of a cabinetmaker, was born in New York City. When his father died in 1865, Charles was forced to seek employment and worked first as an errand boy and then as an employee of a machine shop. At the age of sixteen, he entered the foundry business, while pursuing his passion for acting in evening classes at the Cooper Union.

In 1872 Rohlfs began to design cast-iron stoves and furnaces, though he still aspired to the theater. His acting, however, came to a virtual halt as a result of his courtship of a young novelist and playwright, Anna Katharine Green, whose staid Victorian parents "didn't care much for actors, particularly in the family." The two young people parted company, but their paths crossed again a few years later. The courtship was revived and the Greens consented this time to the marriage, for Rohlfs had in the meantime forsaken his acting career and reverted to his activities as a draughtsman. The couple were accordingly married in November 1884 and moved the following year to Buffalo, where Charles had accepted the managership of a local foundry.

Some years later, probably in 1889 or 1890, he began in his free time to design and manufacture a range of furniture for his home in the Mission style of the time. Soon friends commissioned pieces and Rohlfs's avocation

13   *Fall-front Desk, designed by Charles Rohlfs (1898–1900).*
White oak, iron, and brass. In the Gothic style, the fall-front opens to a writing surface, twin drawers, and shelves above a lower panel pierced with 3 abstract organic motifs. The swollen triangular sides are decorated with a scrolling pattern in brass nails above 4 drawers on the right and a hinged panel on the left which opens to 4 shallow shelves. The piece is accented throughout with brass nailheads and steel hinges. The desk revolves on its base. 56in. (142.2cm.) high; 25½in. (64.8cm.) wide; 23¾in. (60.3cm.) deep. Collection of The Virginia Museum of Fine Arts, Richmond, Virginia. Gift of Sydney and Frances Lewis

blossomed into a home industry. An article in the *Buffalo Times* of 17 February 1905 noted that

His workroom was for seven years in the attic of his residence and many a handsome piece of furniture has been turned out by the workers in the unpretentious attic shop. Seven years ago he opened a shop in the downtown business section and by this time the name and fame of Charles Rohlfs, art furniture maker, has spread far beyond the walls of his own home.

His progress toward a distinct, individual style and the increase in his output had been rapid. By 1902 he was sufficiently well known to be the only American cabinetmaker invited to the Turin Exposition of Decorative Arts. A further honor was afforded him by membership of the Royal Society of Arts in London. Orders flowed in, and Rohlfs moved his workshop to 507–509 Ellicott Street. By 1909 he had eight artisans to execute his designs, first as maquettes, and then, after his approval, in full scale. Nothing is known of these cabinetmakers beyond the name of one, George Thiele. Rohlfs retired from business in the 1920s.

Among Rohlfs's best early pieces is a fall-front desk (13), produced around 1898, in the Gothic style. An almost identical model, differing apparently only in the fretwork design on the front lower panel, was included by Rohlfs in an exhibition at Marshall Field & Co., Chicago, in 1899. Charlotte Moffitt wrote in *House Beautiful*,

In the collection shown in Chicago of this queer, dark, crude, mediaeval furniture is a desk, a very marvel of complexity, with endless delights in the way of doors, pigeon-holes, shelves, and drawers. The drawers and shelves can be pulled out and the doors opened; and while it is not exactly as if they were adjusted with ball-bearings, they work surely, and with as much smoothness as is in keeping with the general effect. When closed – that is when the writing shelf is raised and fastened with its rough hasp of dark steel and crude wooden pin – all the drawers and shelves in place, and the doors closed, it looks like nothing so much as a miniature Swiss cottage. The opposite side from the writing-shelf is a support for books, and the whole desk revolves upon its base.[10]

The reason for Rohlfs's designing the desk to swivel is not recorded, but it is likely that this feature was intended to allow the user to reach for items not only in the side drawers and shelves, but also in the bookshelf on the reverse, while remaining seated. The device is typical of the late-Victorian American cabinetmakers' preoccupation with making furniture multifunctional. Many of these concoctions (as extreme as a piano which contained a bed) are seen in retrospect as marketing gimmicks.

Rohlfs's desk is exceptionally well crafted, even by his high standards. In addition to its neat dowel construction, elaborate carving, and fretwork cutouts, it incorporates on the upper side panels two engaging decorative effects: a scrolling design of nailheads and a hand-hammered finish to the wood's surface, a technique traditionally associated with metalwork and rarely seen on wood.

After the exhibition at Marshall Field's, which included a desk which Mr. Field is reported to have bought for the unprecedented price of $1,000, Rohlfs participated in exhibitions in Buffalo (1901), Turin (1902), and St. Louis (1904). He received private commissions from two reigning monarchs

14   Desk and Chair, designed by Charles Rohlfs (c.1900).
Oak and leather. The desk has 2 rear posts from which are suspended a gallery enclosing 12 drawers and lower pigeonholes. The broad writing surface is supported by twin pedestal feet enclosing further drawers and centering a knee hole with a frieze drawer. The swivel chair has a pierced back flanked by scrolled supports, and flat arm rests. It is upholstered with a strapped leather cushioned back and seat. Both pieces are deeply carved throughout with conventionalized Rohlfs ornamentation. Desk: 72in. (182.9cm.) high; 57in. (144.8cm.) wide; 36in. (91.4cm.) deep. Chair: 36in. (91.4cm.) high; 29in. (73.7cm.) wide; 22in. (55.9cm.) deep. The Manney Collection

– the Kings of Great Britain and Italy – as well as a number of affluent clients from Bremen to Chicago to Canada.

Among his finest pieces is a desk and chair in oak and leather (14) of about 1900. The desk has two rear posts from which is suspended a gallery enclosing twelve drawers and lower pigeonholes above a broad writing surface supported by twin pedestal feet. These in turn enclose further drawers and a kneehole with a frieze drawer. The swivel chair has a pierced back flanked by scrolled supports and flat armrests; it has four curved feet and is upholstered with a strapped leather cushioned back and seat. Both the desk and chair are deeply carved throughout with conventionalized Rohlfs ornamentation.

In the same period he produced an uncharacteristically plain side chair (16) and a rocking chair (15), both in wood. The side chair has a plank back with an angled rectangular shoulder rest above a rectangular seat.

As for the rocking chair (15), it has an elongated back which comprises a central plank rest pierced with three stylized plant motifs. The legs and supports are carved with elaborate fretwork decoration.

Rohlfs's Art Nouveau stylizations – of which his library table of 1904 (17) is a prime example – evolved from the parent movement in Belgium and France at the turn of the century. His sinuous and whiplash silhouettes are drawn directly from the organic attenuations of Horta and Guimard. Rohlfs was presumably exposed to their work in magazines such as *Art et Décoration* and *L'Art Décoratif*, and during his participation at the Turin Exposition. Some of Rohlfs's motifs also echo, in their compact and tangled luxuriance, the architectural ornamentation on Louis Sullivan's Guaranty Insurance Building in downtown Buffalo. The Arts and Crafts Movement, both the English School and its offshoot in New York State, provided yet another influence. Among other designers, Rohlfs was well acquainted with Elbert Hubbard in nearby East Aurora, and he lectured to the Roycrofters on several occasions. His earliest furniture-making essays represented precisely the zeal and idealism preached by Hubbard.[11]

In 1900 Rohlfs produced an elegant side chair of oak (18, 19) with a U-shaped seat resting on four front and two back legs linked by a central stretcher. His preference for oak and ash over other woods evolved from their distinctive grains, which often determined the fanciful motifs with which he embellished the wood's surface. As he noted in a 1901 article in *House Beautiful*, "I owe to the natural lines in wood the inspiration for many an effective design. While they are far removed from direct imitation, yet the impetus came from the grain of ash wood."[12]

His rocking chair of about 1910–12 (20) is another example of oak, this time with leather. An almost identical chair, varying only in its design of the terminals on the armrests and the addition of a padded back rest, was among the furniture in Rohlfs's own home.[13] The addition of an oriental motif to the basic Arts and Crafts shape of this chair is typical of the artistic license which the self-taught Rohlfs brought to his work. Few of his contemporaries would have attempted to combine potentially conflicting styles in such an unconventional manner.

A waste-basket of 1905–10 (21) shows how Rohlfs could transform a potentially nondescript piece of household furniture into one which

15   Rocking Chair, designed by Charles
Rohlfs (1901).
*Oak. The elongated back comprises a central
plank rest pierced with 3 stylized plant motifs
beneath extending scrolled supports. The
square drop-in cushioned seat (reupholstered)
is supported by legs carved with fretwork
decoration. 52in. (132.1cm.) high; 20in.
(50.8cm.) wide; 18in. (45.8cm.) deep.
Collection of The Carnegie Museum of Art,
Pittsburgh, Pennsylvania.
DuPuy Fund, 1984*

16   Side Chair, designed by Charles Rohlfs
(1900–05).
*Stained ash. The chair has a plank back with
an angled rectangular shoulder-rest above a
rectangular seat. The square legs are joined at
the front and sides by arched aprons, the pegs
with unevenly chamfered finish. 33½in.
(85cm.) high; 15½in. (39.4cm.) wide; 18in.
(45.7cm.) deep.
Collection of Tod M. Volpe*

17   *Library Table, designed by Charles*
Rohlfs (c.1904).
Oak with copper latch and hinges, and leather
top. An octagonal table, with conforming
sides, each decorated with a band of pierced
fretwork motifs. Two sides form a door which
opens to two shelves. 30in. (76.2cm.)
high;31⅞in. (81cm.) diameter.
Collection of Mr. and Mrs. John M. Angelo

Right and below

18, 19　Side Chair, and detail, designed by
Charles Rohlfs (1900).
Oak. The backrest has a carved and pierced
center section decorated with elongated leaf
and stem motifs beneath tall slender supports
headed by S-carved finials. The U-shaped seat
rests on 4 front and 2 back legs linked by a
central stretcher. 57in. (144cm.) high;
18⅞in. (48cm.) maximum width.
Private Collection

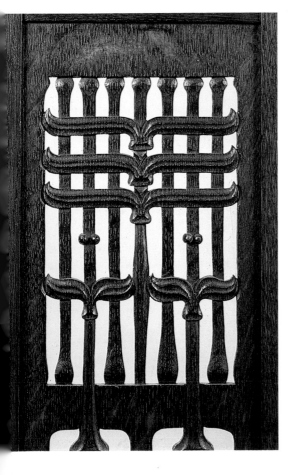

20   Rocking Chair, designed by Charles Rohlfs (1910–12).
Oak and leather. The broad back has an angled crest above a square studded and padded green leather seat. In the center of the sides are circular panels pierced with an Oriental motif. 31in. (78.7cm.) high; 24in. (61cm.) wide; 17½in. (44.5cm.) depth of seat.
Collection of Susan Fetterolf and Jeffrey Gorrin

21 Waste-basket, designed and executed by Charles Rohlfs (1905–10).
Oak and leather. The 4 posts, headed by flame finials, suspend a leather basket from iron rings. The lower sides are composed of arched panels pierced with oval cut-outs. 30in. (76.2cm.) high; 15in. (38.1cm.) wide; 15in. (38.1cm.)deep.
Collection of David and Beth Cathers

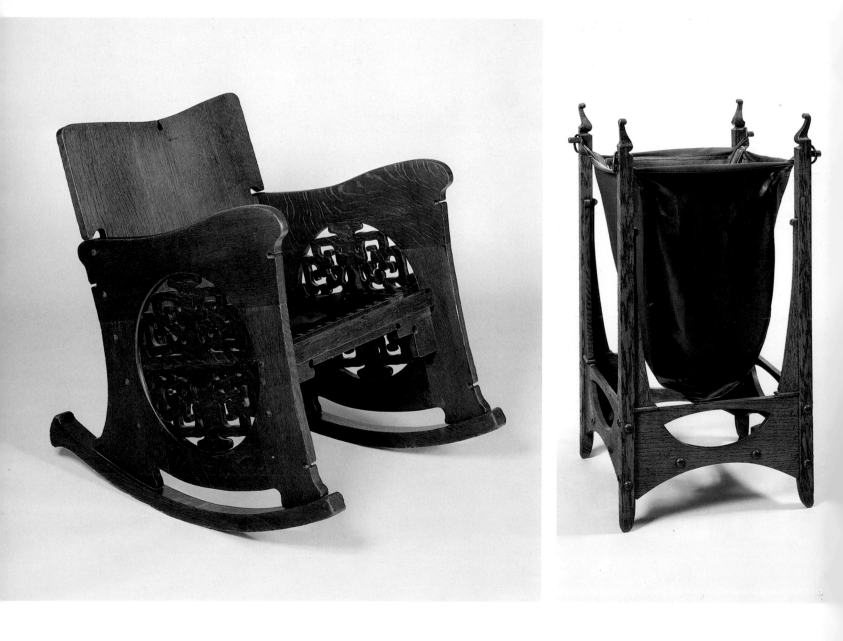

imparts a feeling of playfulness and romance by the incorporation of small flame-like finials.

Although the influences on Rohlfs's style are obvious, his work shows an energetic blend of whimsy, functionalism, and solid handcrafting that was unmistakably his own. He is seen today as neither a pioneer nor a full disciple, but as an excellent craftsman with an originality that is immediately identifiable.

Frank Lloyd Wright

Frank Lloyd Wright's relationship to the Arts and Crafts Movement, both indigenous and European, was not a simple one. Like William Morris and John Ruskin, whose reformist beliefs generated a resurgence of handicraft ideals when the negative aspects of the Industrial Revolution manifested themselves in late-Victorian England, Wright was in favor of simple unadorned forms. He differed sharply, however, in how these should be achieved. As he stated in the famous speech, "The Art and Craft of the Machine," which he addressed to the Chicago Arts and Crafts Society at Hull House on 6 March 1901, "William Morris pleaded well for simplicity as the basis of all true art. Let us understand the significance to art of the word – SIMPLICITY – for it is vital to the Art of the Machine."[14]

The Arts and Crafts philosophy at the turn of the century remained locked into the handicraft ideal: in order to be "honest," an item had to be handmade. Wright never came to terms with the Mission furniture of the Stickleys, Charles Rohlfs, and others. It was not incompatible with his interiors, but he felt intellectually superior to it; in its rudimentary construction it was conceptually a remnant of the nineteenth century, whereas his, made by machine, was firmly in the twentieth. The British designer C.R. Ashbee, who shared Wright's design esthetic but not his belief in the machine to achieve it, quoted Wright as saying, "My God . . . is machinery, and the art of the future will be the expression of the individual artist through the thousand powers of the machine, the machine doing all those things that the individual workman cannot do, and the creative artist is the man that controls all this and understands it."[15]

Wright proved to be correct in his anticipation of the machine's future, but his refusal to acknowledge the impact of the Arts and Crafts Movement on his own evolving furniture style is readily disputed. An examination of contemporary periodicals, such as *The Studio*, and, in the U.S.A., *House Beautiful* and *The Western Architect*, to which Wright had access, shows that architects and designers such as Mackintosh, Voysey, Gimson, and Ashbee introduced furniture with ladderback, spindle, and splat components before Wright's own productions. There was clearly borrowing on both sides of the Atlantic, so Wright's later claim that "No practice by any European architect to this day has influenced mine in the least" was not only mean-spirited and unchivalrous, but patently untrue.[16]

What is characteristic of Wright is the fact that virtually all his furniture was intended for use in the specific house for which it was designed. Although a great deal of it – such as cabinets, bookcases, and benches – was built-in, as part of Wright's pursuit of an organic and fully integrated

Below

22   High-back Dining Chair, designed by Frank Lloyd Wright for the Ward Winfield Willits house, Highland Park, Chicago (c.1902).
*Oak with green leather drop-in seat. The back has 11 spindles beneath a broad crest-rail flanked by slightly angled tapering supports with backward-curving terminals and rear feet. The square seat is raised on square front feet, linked by an H-stretcher. 56in. (142.3cm.) high.
Collection of The Metropolitan Museum of Art, New York. Purchase, Mr. and Mrs. David Lubart. Gift, in memory of Katherine J. Lubart, 1944–1975, 1978. Photo Frances McLaughlin-Gill c.1982*

Right above

23   Spindle Armchair, designed by Frank Lloyd Wright for the Dana house, Springfield, Illinois (c.1903).
*Oak with upholstery. Each of the 3 sides has 9 spindles. 22in. (55.8cm.) high; 26in. (66cm.) wide; 22.5in. (57.1cm.) deep.
The Dana-Thomas House. The Illinois Historic Preservation Agency. Photo Photographic Services Corporation.*

Right below

24   Spindle Armchair, designed by Frank Lloyd Wright for the Dana house, Springfield, Illinois (c.1903).
*Oak with upholstery. A pentagonal chair, each side with 9 spindles. 24in. (61cm.) high; 24³⁄₁₆in. (61.4cm.) wide; 22½in. (57.1cm.) deep.
The Dana-Thomas House. The Illinois Historic Preservation Agency. Photo Photographic Services Corporation.*

interior space, his freestanding furniture played a vital role in this attempt to achieve a unified architectural environment. Each chair, like the room's ceilings, walls, and windows, is therefore a reaffirmation of the house's overall matrix of design. An important example, his high-back dining chair of oak with green leather drop-in seat (22) was designed around 1902 for the Ward Winfield Willits house in Highland Park, Chicago. It is important for two reasons: first, because it was designed for Wright's first mature Prairie house, and second, because, in multiple, it performed a special function within that interior. Gathered around the dining table, the set of high-back chairs formed an enclosure that created a special space for the social ceremony of eating. The screened effect imparts a sense of warmth and intimacy. Although the design of the individual chairs is dignified and disciplined, its sharp rectilinearity allows no concession to the human anatomy, leaving some observers today to speculate on the discomfort endured by the original corseted wives and their guests who had to maintain an upright posture of near military proportions throughout the lengthy ritual of a turn-of-the-century repast (many years later, Wright admitted that he had approached furniture design from a cultural stand-point, rather than from one of comfort).

The Willits chair's simple elegance is repeated in Wright's models for other Prairie School houses, such as for the P.A. Beachy house in 1906 in Oak Park. On developing a successful chair design, Wright proposed it, with slight modifications, to different clients. Each model is a subtle variation on a common architectural theme.

Willits, a Chicagoan by birth, wrote to Wright after reading the catalogue of Wright's Chicago Architectural Club exhibition in 1902. By January 1903 construction of the Willits house was well under way. The family moved into the house in May, before the final stages had been reached. Its completion marked Wright's first Prairie School masterpiece.

In the same period, Wright was engaged to remodel the Dana-Thomas house in Springfield, Illinois. What started out, however, as a project of minor alterations developed into a total renovation; the original house was leveled (except for one room, which still exists). Begun in the Spring of 1902, this renovation was completed in November, 1904. The house was lived in by a member of the original family until 1942, sold in 1944, and since 1981 has been the property of the State of Illinois, under whose aegis restoration has been taking place.

The spindle armchair Wright designed for the Dana house (23) is made of oak with upholstery, and there are two examples in the house. It is a three-sided chair, each side having nine spindles. The spindled arms and backs recall similar models by some of Wright's contemporaries, particularly Gustav Stickley. Another similar spindle armchair (24) in the Dana house has five sides, each with multiple spindles.

All the furniture in the Dana house was constructed of white oak, to which was applied a reddish-brown stain manufactured by the Johnson Wax Company of Racine, Wisconsin. One of Wright's most famous later buildings was commissioned by that company.

Around 1903 Wright designed an extremely beautiful print table (25) which was used later in the house he built between 1908 and 1913 for Mr.

Opposite

25 *Print Table, designed by Frank Lloyd Wright for Mr. and Mrs. Francis Little, Wayzata, Minnesota (c.1903).*
Oak. The top is hinged in the center so that it can be folded upright and lowered into the fitted section between the two posts. 45⅜in. (115.2cm.) high; 44 1/16 in. (112cm.) wide. Collection of The Metropolitan Museum of Art. Purchase, Emily Crane Chadbourne Bequest, 1972. Photo Frances McLaughlin-Gill c.1982

Below left

26 *Side Chair, designed, by Frank Lloyd Wright for the Larkin Administration Building, Buffalo, New York (c.1904). Oak with leather upholstery. The angled plank back extends from above the crest-rail to the rear stretcher. The square padded drop-in seat is supported by rectangular feet 40¼in. (102.2cm.) high; 14⅞in. (37.8cm.) wide; 18¼in. (46.3cm.) deep. Lent by Daniel Wolf, 1986. Courtesy of The Metropolitan Museum of Art, New York*

Below right

27 *Tall-back Side Chair, designed by Frank Lloyd Wright for the Edward Everett Boynton house, Rochester, New York (1908). American white oak with drop-in upholstered seat. The plank back has vertical supports which extend to terminals above a horizontal crest-rail and decorative molding. The cushioned seat is supported by square feet continuing to gently outcurved toes. 48in. (122cm.) high; 15½in. (39.5cm.) wide. Collection of Mr. and Mrs. Milton Brechner*

and Mrs. Francis Little in Wayzata, Minnesota. The top of the table is hinged in the center so that it can be folded upright and lowered into the fitted section between the two posts for storage purposes. The four spindled gateleg supports likewise fold into the center. The horizontal moldings on the posts and gateleg supports are typical of the furniture ornamentation of Wright's early Prairie houses, and this suggests that the table was designed for the earlier house which Wright built for the Littles in Peoria, Illinois, in 1902. The Wayzata house was lived in by members of the Little family until it had to be demolished in 1972. At that time The Metropolitan Museum of Art, New York, bought the entire house and installed the living room in the American Wing of the museum.

The Larkin Administration Building in Buffalo was Wright's first commercial structure; it met with considerable criticism, despite its revolutionary designs for new systems for fireproofing, heating, ventilation, lighting, plumbing, and pneumatic cleaning. One of the pieces of furniture that Wright installed in the building was an oak side chair with leather upholstery (26). With slight modifications, Wright incorporated this model into at least three other interiors: his own home and studio in Oak Park, the Hillside Home School in Spring Green, Wisconsin, and the Unity Temple in Oak Park. Although it was clearly one of Wright's favorite models, its suitability for the Larkin Administration Building is questionable. The architect responded to the Larkin commission with an extremely innovative range of metal furnishings, all carefully designed to provide optimum working conditions and hygiene in a commercial space. Materials such as magnesite were introduced to facilitate overnight cleaning and to ensure durability. The inclusion of the oak chair in this avant-garde office setting therefore appears somewhat incongruous. Its simple Arts and Crafts form and wood construction were far better suited to Wright's warm Prairie House interiors.

The tall-back side chair designed by Wright in 1908 for the Edward Everett Boynton house in Rochester, New York (27), was a model which he adapted with subtle variations for a set of dining room chairs in the house. In particular, the crest-rail of the dining room chairs is broader, and the horizontal molding is transferred to the lower half.

In the same year, Wright used the horizontal molding on this chair's crest-rail for the furniture he designed for the Isabel Roberts house in River Forest. Within two years such moldings had disappeared from Wright's decorative vocabulary, as had the terminals on the chair back. His models became increasingly plain, their contours less ornamented.

The chair's plank back evolved from the model Wright introduced in 1904 for both the Larkin building and his own studio in Oak Park. He had begun gradually to replace his earlier slatted chair models with solid backs, partly as a concession to the greater facility of construction and the reduced expense.

By 1912–14, when he designed a library table (28) specifically for the Francis W. Little house in Wayzata, its uncomplicated planes represented a sharp stylistic departure from the delicacy of his earlier furniture designs.[17] Produced after his return from Europe in 1911, it indicates that the overseas sojourn had sparked off an evolution in his design philosophy; this can be

seen also in his furnishings for Taliesin at Spring Green (1911). David A. Hanks, in *The Decorative Designs of Frank Lloyd Wright*, observes that "The darker-stained furniture of the Prairie years was replaced by unstained oak furniture that was lighter; the horizontal molding was abandoned; and the terminals of the vertical elements were eliminated. Forms were more straightforward and severely geometric and were often 'hung' from four square posts to allow for the spatial flow and to lighten the appearance of a strong form."[18] In many ways, therefore, this table represents the summation of all Wright's earlier concepts with a view to what lay ahead in his Usonian period, which began in 1937. The only concession to ornament on the table is the stepped edge of the rectangular top. Even the traditional use of handles or pulls for the cupboard doors has been abandoned in preference for small apertures which serve as handles. Comparison of this library table with the other piece of furniture from the Wayzata home (25) shows unequivocally that they were conceived at different times in the architect's career.

Roycroft

The founding of the Roycroft Furniture Shop in East Aurora, New York, was almost accidental. Copies of pieces made by local carpenters for the Roycroft Inn were ordered by guests, a demand which led to a line of eleven models in the firm's 1901 catalogue. The pieces were heavy and simple, drawing their inspiration from the prevailing Mission style. An article in *House Beautiful* in 1901 described a side chair, model no. 031 (31), as "honest and simple enough in construction, but somewhat too austere in design, and altogether too massive to be pleasing."[19] Although refinements were introduced, the model's principal qualities remain its solid and severe structure which, combined with the bold lettering of the signature, exemplify the pride and diligence which Roycroft placed in its workmanship, and which its idealistic head, Elbert Hubbard, described in one of his epigrams: "made the best we know how."

In its 1906 catalogue, the Roycroft Shop offered a cellarette, model no. 019 (29), in one of three woods: oak ($42), mahogany ($50), and ash ($40). A slightly larger model without drawers was offered in the identical range of woods at slightly lower prices. The designer of the cellarette is unrecorded. The principal furniture designer in the early years of Roycroft was Victor Toothacker, whose signed pen-and-ink furniture sketches appear in the firm's furniture catalogue and pamphlets. Other cabinetmakers, whose ideas were occasionally translated into finished pieces, included Herbert Buffum, William Roth, James Cadzow, Tom Standeven, and Albert Danner. Of these, Cadzow and Roth, who both also participated in the construction of the buildings in the Roycroft village, contributed important furniture designs. None of these, however, was allowed individual credit by Hubbard. Roycroft furniture bears only the firm's orb-and-cross logo and/or its name in carved lettering.

A designer particularly associated with Roycroft was Dard Hunter, and it seems likely that a bookcase/magazine stand of about 1906 (30) was designed while he was there.[20] A matching chair, with a broad back splat

29 *Cellarette, model no.019, executed at the Roycroft Shops (pre-1906).*
Oak and copper. The cupboard doors open to an interior fitted on one door with a revolving tray for bottles and glasses, and on the other with an ice bucket. With hand-wrought copper handle plates and hinges. 34in (86.3cm.) high; 40⅛in. (102cm.) wide; 19⅝in. (49.8cm.) deep.
Collection of Tazio Nuvolari

30   Bookcase/Magazine Stand, designed by
Dard Hunter, the Roycroft Shops (c.1906).
American white oak, stained black. The 4
shelves are attached with accentuated mortice
and tenon joints. 45¾in. (126.2cm.) high;
32½in. (82.5cm.) wide; 11¹⁵⁄₁₆in. (30.3cm.)
deep.
Private Collection

31   Side Chair, model no. 031, executed at
the Roycroft Shops (1900–05).
American white oak, quarter sawn. The 3
vertical back splats are flanked by tapering
square supports above a flaring square seat.
46⅞in. (119cm.) high; 17³⁄₁₆in. (43.7cm.)
wide; 18¹⁵⁄₁₆in. (48.1cm.) deep.
*Courtesy of The Metropolitan Museum of
Art. Ex-collection Robert Blasberg through
the courtesy of the Jordan-Volpe Gallery.
1984*

similarly carved with the inscription "Sit down and rest thy weary bones," remained in the Hunter family for many years.[21] A letter from Hunter to his previous employer, the *Chillicothe News-Advertiser*, on 2 August 1904 – three weeks after his arrival in East Aurora – was full of his enthusiasm for Roycroft's furniture, which he felt was "the most beautiful because it is the simplest furniture, and is made by artists and not by mechanics and machines. It is solid and just what it appears to be – no shams, no veneer. It is good, plain, strong, artistic." The robust construction of his bookcase, with its oversized joints, shows Hunter's easy facility with the Roycroft handcraft philosophy. Considering the degree to which he involved himself with every medium in which he worked, it is likely that Hunter carved and assembled this piece on his own.

Purcell, Feick & Elmslie

George Grant Elmslie was born in Aberdeenshire, Scotland, in 1871, and received his only formal education at the Duke of Gordon School before emigrating to the U.S.A. He began his architectural apprenticeship in the office of William LeBaron Jenney; then transferred, with his fellow trainee Frank Lloyd Wright, to the office of Joseph Lyman Silsbee. In 1889 he joined the important Chicago firm of Adler & Sullivan as a draughtsman, and in 1896 he was promoted to chief designer. His responsibilities in that position included the execution of Sullivan's ornamental designs. In 1909 he left to join Purcell and Feick.[22]

Ten years Elmslie's junior, William Gray Purcell was born in 1880 in Oak Park, Illinois.[23] He was raised by his grandfather, William Cunningham Gray, the editor and publisher of the newspaper *The Interior*. After formal schooling, he obtained a degree in architecture from Cornell University. During a trip to Europe, he became interested in Secessionist architecture, and on his return to the U.S.A. he served his apprenticeship in various architectural firms – including Adler & Sullivan, where he worked briefly under Elmslie, and John Gallen Howard in Berkeley, California – before establishing his own firm in 1906 in partnership with a former Cornell classmate, George Feick.

In 1912, the firm was retained to design the Edison Shop, a phonograph company, for the Babson brothers. At the same time Henry B. Babson commissioned Elmslie to design eight additional pieces of furniture for the house in Riverside, Illinois, which Elmslie had collaborated on in 1907 while in Sullivan's office. Included in this commission were arm- and side-chairs, tables, andirons and a tall-case clock (32). This clock is in the mature Prairie School style; for Elmslie it is relatively unembellished and architectonic, showing less of Sullivan's influence and more of Wright's, than most of his furniture designs. The lower central openwork panel provides a reminder of Elmslie's earlier style, with its clear influence of Sullivan's work in the use of ornamentation. The slender case, however, echoes Wright, particularly in the set of horizontal fins on the upper terminals, which Elmslie incorporated also into his furnishings for the Edward W. Decker residence in Minneapolis in the same year. The effect is serene and dignified, far more restrained than Elmslie's average piece of furniture.

Elmslie and Purcell enjoyed an extremely close collaborative relationship for fifteen years (only seven of which were spent directly in partnership). It is therefore often difficult, it not impossible, to attribute the design of an object to one or the other of them. The armchair designed for the Merchants Bank of Winona, Minnesota, in 1912–13 (34) provides an example of this problem. Its abrupt contours, tight composition, and virtual lack of ornamentation point to Purcell as much as to Elmslie, a fact borne out by an office memo in Elmslie's handwriting, dated 6 April 1913, concerning the design of the chairs for the Merchants Bank. It states, in part, "The Winona chairs are the toughest kind of a problem to get comfort and appearance with the present basis. I have been trying all kinds of variants from your sketches and really feel that a cushion panel back rest is the best of them all, only I would make it as wide as we possibly can. I feel that a narrow effect is sort of apologetic while if we make it wide it will appear more natural and not disengage the corners of the back so much ..." In another notation Elmslie wrote, "You *have* to do a little thinking on the chairs – they are *not* comfortable and must be made so. 4"–5" will do it but how without narrowing the seat?"[24]

The chair's high angled back and extended seat provide the comfort that Elmslie sought. In this respect it is more successful than the spindle cube chair models which Wright had earlier designed for some of his Prairie style houses and which one must assume served as prototypes for this model.

The vacation home which Purcell and Elmslie designed in 1912–13 for Edward Williams Decker on Lake Minnetonka, Minnesota, contained a table (33) which was attributed to Purcell on the original billing sheet for the house (now in the collection of the Minnesota Historical Society). Included in the furnishings were several architectural elements (for example, newel posts and dining room chairs) which incorporated a set of horizontal fins in the upper terminals. These resemble those on the tall-case clock for which Elmslie has been credited (32) – a fact which further indicates how difficult it is to distinguish between Elmslie's and Purcell's designs.

In 1913 Feick resigned from the firm, leaving Purcell and Elmslie in partnership until 1922, a loose but practical arrangement which survived moves by Purcell to both Philadelphia and Oregon. Their most productive period was 1910–15, during which they designed a large number of residences in Minnesota and Wisconsin. Like many architects of the time, they involved themselves in the broad spectrum of design, including furniture, landscaping, and fabrics. Unlike most, however, they placed considerable emphasis on ornament as a means of achieving harmony and rhythm.

George Washington Maher

George Washington Maher (1864–1926) was born in Mill Creek, West Virginia, but later moved to Chicago.[25] After a brief apprenticeship in the offices of Bauer and Hill, he transferred to J.L. Silsbee, where he gained the greater part of his training and developed the influences seen in his early work. Here, also, he first stated his theories on architecture in a paper read

35 *Armchair, designed by George Washington Maher (1911–12). Oak with studded and padded leather upholstery. Designed for the reception room of "Rockledge," the summer home of Mr. Ernest L. King, near Homer, Winona County, Minnesota. Of throne-like shape and proportions, the chair has an arched Gothic crest-rail above a central serpentine upholstered backrest between a pair of splats headed by wedge-shaped dentilled capitals. The square seat is similarly upholstered between pierced sides continuing in the front and rear to flaring legs resting on block feet. 58¹¹⁄₁₆in. (149.1cm.) high; 33in. (83.8cm.) wide; 26½in. (67.3cm.) deep. The Metropolitan Museum of Art, New York. Purchase, Theodore R. Gamble, Jr. Gift, in honor of his mother, Mrs. Theodore Robert Gamble, 1982*

before the Architectural Sketch Club on 12 September 1887, "Originality in American Architecture." In 1888 Maher opened his own office. Around 1892 he took a trip to Europe to cure a severe nervous disorder and at the same time to complete his architectural education. On returning to Chicago, he began a practice which continued uninterrupted for the next thirty years. By 1900 Maher's office was handling a significant number of commissions, most of them residential. During the years 1908–12 he reached the height of his success, receiving two large commissions: a new gymnasium and a science building for Northwestern University in Evanston.

Maher's most important client in the 1910–20 decade was the J.R. Watkins Company of Winona. It was for the President of this company, Mr. Ernest L. King, and his wife, that he designed "Rockledge," a large Prairie School residence situated at the base of a limestone bluff on the west bank of the Mississippi River. Rockledge included a central bungalow consisting of twenty-eight rooms on three floors, a garage, and a horse barn. The buildings were distinctly Oriental in style, reflecting the Kings' love of the Far East; and a Japanese landscape architect, Otsuka, was retained to design complementary grounds.

Rockledge provided Maher with ample opportunity to incorporate his motif-rhythm theory of decoration, the fundamental principle of which he described as being "to receive the dominant inspiration from the patron, taking into strict account his needs, his temperament, and environment, influenced by local color and atmosphere in surrounding flora and nature. With these vital impressions at hand, the design naturally crystallizes and motifs appear which being consistently utilized will make each object, whether it be of construction, furniture, or decoration, related ..." An armchair of oak with studded and padded leather upholstery (35), designed by Maher for "Rockledge," includes three decorative motifs which recur, with variations, throughout the house, in both its architectural and furniture ornamentation: the wedge-shaped tripartite dentil capital, the arched crest-rail (generally described as a segmental pediment), and, most significantly, the tapering form of the legs and stiles, which matched the house's Orientally inspired slanted walls. Other influences are also apparent in the chair's design: its spoon back evokes the early American Queen Anne style, while the canted tops of the legs and stiles recall furniture models by C.F.A. Voysey. Another unifying design element within the house (not incorporated here) was an indigenous coral-colored lily which the architect repeated in its fabrics, stained glass panels, and light fixtures in a manner similar to that which he had used in his house for James Patten of 1897 (thistles) and his Harry Rubens house of 1902–03 (hollyhocks).

Greene and Greene

The excitement of the Greenes' furniture – its design, execution and choice of ebony as a contrasting inlay – drew the praise of C.R. Ashbee. On visiting Charles Greene in his workshop in 1909, Ashbee wrote of "the best and most characteristic furniture I have seen in this country. There were beautiful cabinets and chairs of walnut and lignum-vitae, exquisite

36 Armchair, designed by Greene and Greene for the living room of the Robert R. Blacker house, Pasadena, California, executed by John Hall (1907–09). Mahogany, ebony, mother-of-pearl, copper, and silver, with replaced upholstery. The curved crest-rail has ebony pegs; the serpentine open armrests are joined to the front legs by ebony splines; the apron is braced below by openwork Chinese cloud-form brackets. 33¼in. (84.4cm.) high; 24³⁄₁₆in. (61.4cm.) wide; 19³⁄₁₆in. (48.7cm.) deep. Property of Max Palevsky. Photo York Photographic Design, Los Angeles, California

37   Hall Cabinet, designed by Greene and
Greene for the Robert R. Blacker house,
Pasadena, California, executed by John Hall
(1907–09).
*Teak and ebony. The rectangular top above 2
graduating drawers is flanked by cupboard
doors crisply carved and inlaid with reversing
panels of trees in a cloudy landscape. 36⁹/₁₆in.
(92.8cm.) high; 60¹¹/₁₆in. (154.1cm.) wide;
20³/₄in. (52.6cm.) deep.
Property of Max Palevsky, Photo York
Photographic Design, Los Angeles, California*

doweling and pegging, and in all a supreme feeling for material, quite up to the best of our English craftsmanship …."[26] With hindsight, one can state unequivocally that the Greenes' cabinetry exceeded anything done at the time in either England or Europe.

A mahogany and ebony armchair and a hall cabinet in teak (36, 37) were designed for the Robert R. Blacker house in Pasadena, and were executed by John Hall. The complexity of design in the armchair, one of two made, required masterly cabinetry skills. The crest-rail, rear legs (at the top), and armrests all consist of elements that move in two planes simultaneously; the armrests, for example, arch upwards and extend outwards at the same time. The pair of undulating splines which hold the arms and legs together are another important structural element in this chair. They are influenced by a Chinese household form of decoration known as "lift," which is a linear abstraction of a cloud form. The motif repeats itself in the openwork brackets which brace the front chair legs.

The Blacker house, for which the pieces were made, launched the Greenes' reputation in Pasadena. Within a few years they were in the vanguard of the new California movement in architecture. Built at a cost exceeding $1,000,000, the house was the most elaborate of the Greenes' commissions, combining a rich array of influences, primarily Oriental.

Robert Blacker was a retired lumberman from Michigan. He had been drawn to the Greenes on a visit to their neighborhood overlooking the Arroyo Sec, when he saw several heavy-timbered bungalows they had built. He and his wife were friends of the Gambles, and the Gamble house followed almost immediately. Then came residences for Charles M. Pratt and William R. Thorsen. These established fully the Greenes' reputation as pioneers of a highly distinctive and creative native American architecture achieved in large part by its exuberant Arts and Crafts cabinetry.

John Hall was widely considered to be the finest cabinetmaker on the West Coast. The Greenes, too, and particularly Charles, were themselves highly accomplished woodworkers from their years at the Washington University Manual Training High School. The production of their interiors – chairs, light fixtures, wall paneling, and so on – therefore became a joint Greene-Hall venture. Charles spent two to three hours each day supervising production.

The Blacker house was owned by the family from 1907 to 1943, after which it appears to have remained unoccupied for some years until purchased by Max and Marjorie Hill, who lived in it until 1983. The following year it was purchased by Barton English, who removed the light fixtures (some 53 in all). A local ordinance was passed to prevent the removal of further fittings, such as windows and doors. The house is at present unoccupied.

Arthur Mathews and Lucia Kleinhans Mathews

Arthur Mathews (1860–1945) was born in Markesan, Wisconsin. The family later settled in San Francisco, where, in 1875, Mathews apprenticed as an architectural draftsman in his father's office.[27] After various designer and illustrator jobs between 1881 and 1884, Mathews went in 1885 to

38 Fall-front Desk, designed and executed by Arthur Mathews and Lucia Kleinhans Mathews, the Furniture Shop (1910–20). Carved and painted wood, and brass. Exterior of the fall-front, carved and painted with a Renaissance harvest scene within foliate borders intersected by oval figural medallions. The desk itself has a rectangular top shelf above an open shelf supported by front carved crouching figures. The fall-front opens to a fitted interior with drawers and central well painted with the figure of a woman. The sides also have carved and painted panels. Desk: 59in. (149.9cm.) high; 48in. (122cm.) wide; 20in. (50.8cm.) deep. Collection of The Oakland Museum, Oakland, California. Gift of Concours d'Antiques, Art Guild; The Oakland Museum Association

Paris, studying at the Académie Julian under Gustave Boulanger and Jules Lefebvre. After graduation, he exhibited his paintings both in the Paris Salons and in San Francisco, to which he returned in 1889. In 1890 he was appointed Dean of the School of Design in the Mark Hopkins Institute of Art, and it was while he was there that he married a pupil, Lucia Kleinhans.

Lucia Kleinhans Mathews (1870–1955) was born in San Francisco and studied at the Mark Hopkins Institute of Art. After her marriage to Mathews she began occasionally to display her works with him in local exhibitions. In 1899 the couple left for a European trip during which Arthur opened an atelier in Paris and Lucia attended James Whistler's Académie-Carmen. On returning to San Francisco, she continued to exhibit her paintings sporadically.

Arthur Mathews formed the Furniture Shop in 1906, in association with John Zeile, in large part to meet the demands for furnishings by wealthy San Franciscans in the wake of the earthquake and fire which leveled the city earlier that year. Located at 1717 California Street, the Shop was made up of skilled artisans, carvers, cabinetmakers, and decorators who worked under the direction of Mathews and his chief design assistant, Thomas A. McGlynn. The staff ranged in number from twenty to fifty, matching the flow of work. Lucia Kleinhans Mathews both supervised, and collaborated as both designer and woodcarver on numerous projects including the Savings Union Bank (1911) and the Masonic Temple (1913). A significant part of the Shop's production was geared to relatively unornamented furniture for commercial usage. The Shop closed in 1920, due in part to the decline in work caused by World War I.

A fall-front desk (38) is one of the master works of the Furniture Shop. Its form and ornamentation are drawn both from Renaissance prototypes and the English Victorian revival in the 1880s by artist-decorators such as William Burges. The robust frame emphasizes its dependency on seventeenth-century forms, as does its use of corbel-like carved upper supports, carved and painted side panels, and a fall-front which resembles a framed Old Master painting. The degree of ornamentation, extended with equal attention to the desk's interior, shows a preoccupation with esthetics which recalls the English Arts and Crafts Movement when it gave full interpretation to William Morris's doctrine, "Have nothing in your home which you do not know to be useful or think to be beautiful."

Items produced by the Furniture Shop with this degree of handwork were reserved for prize private or public commissions which allowed Mathews to produce a harmonious interior, one in which the desk would complement stylistically both the other furnishings, wall panelings, and his paintings (and their frames). One must assume that the significance of the desk's motifs would become apparent when viewed in its original setting.[28]

Mathews's preference for traditional furniture forms is also evident in a pair of candlesticks (40). Their fluted spiraling forms evoke the late eighteenth century. His other small decorative objects, such as an hourglass and mantel clock, likewise take their inspiration from French Classicism; in the first instance also Louis XVI, and in the second Directoire.[29] San Franciscans at the turn of the century identified themselves fiercely, in matters of art and culture, with Paris, rather than New York or Munich, an

Below left

39   Lidded Box, designed and executed by Lucia Kleinhans Mathews (1929).
Painted wood. The top is decorated with a profusion of multicolored poppies within a beige border. The sides are painted with landscape panels. 16in. (40.6cm.) long; 5in. (12.7cm.) high; 12in. (30.5cm.) deep. Collection of The Oakland Museum, Oakland, California. Photo Joe Samberg

Below right

40   Pair of Candlesticks, designed and executed by Arthur Mathews and Lucia Kleinhans Mathews, the Furniture Shop (1910–20).
Turned, carved and painted wood, and brass. Each candlestick is of tapering cylindrical form with fluted spirals and painted with flowers rising from a pod-form foot and stepped circular base. 29½in. (75cm.) high. Collection of The Oakland Museum. Gift of the Art Guild. Photo M. Lee Fatherree

affiliation to which Mathews contributed. The candlesticks' floral decoration and lively choice of color transform them, however, into modern creations, far removed from their French forbears. The hand-carved and painted ornamentation combines the skills of both Arthur and Lucia, though in this instance her skills dominate. She had an affinity for small scale detailing which he lacked. Her painting style was also tighter, an advantage in diminutive works such as these. Two pricket candlesticks by the couple in the collection of the Oakland Museum incorporate flower-enveloped maidens in vibrant colors enriched with gold leaf.[30] Items such as these were clearly designed for the custom-made interiors which the Furniture Shop manufactured for opulent clients. Their elaborately painted finish suggested a decorative, rather than a functional, use, as dripping hot candle wax would have discolored, and ultimately destroyed, their surfaces. Typical of what became known as the California Decorative Style, the candlesticks represent a dimension of the American Arts and Crafts Movement far removed from the robust functional examples of Hubbard and Stickley.

Two of Lucia Mathews's principal interests – horticulture and painting – manifested themselves in a range of charming table top items such as lidded jars, picture frames, and clocks. Included was a box (39), in which the central motif is the California poppy painted in a warm, flat decorative style. The lower panels portray another distinct Mathews theme, beloved of both the husband and wife: the California landscape, in this instance probably vignettes of the Monterey peninsula. Lucia designed numerous similar images to enhance the pages of *Philopolis*, the monthly magazine which she and her husband published between 1906 and 1916.

2 *Ceramics*

T he development of a ceramic art in America was significant culturally, artistically and spiritually. Although art and industry reached a high point in the decorative techniques of potteries such as Rookwood, Fulper, Grueby, Gates, and Tiffany, all of whom made their contribution to America's commercial progress, the wares of other potteries remained true to the potter's art and craft. This was reflected in the work of potters such as George Ohr, Hugh Robertson, Adelaide Alsop Robineau, and Theophilus Brouwer. The choice either of experimenting with glaze techniques or concentrating on hand-painted decoration offered a contrasting range of esthetic. By the turn of the century it had become apparent that the United States had taken great strides in the applied arts and that its accomplishments could be compared favorably with those of European and Oriental decorative arts.

Rookwood Pottery

Rookwood, one of America's largest and most important art potteries, was founded in 1880 by Maria Longworth Nichols (1849–1932). Maria Longworth was the granddaughter of Nicholas Longworth, a Cincinnati real estate millionaire. Her father, Joseph Longworth, became a respected patron of the arts and a benefactor of the Cincinnati Art Museum. In 1868 she married George Ward Nichols. Her interest in porcelain grew in the 1870s and in 1875 led to the formation of a committee to promote "the lucrative employment of women" and to raise funds to participate in the Philadelphia Centennial Exposition the following year.[1] The Exposition included a remarkable display of Japanese wares, which had a profound influence on Mrs. Nichols. Her earliest creations at the Rookwood Pottery introduced a range of Japanese themes: spiders in their webs, cranes, flying bats, and so forth. The pottery's first paid decorators were Albert Valentien in 1881, and Matthew Daly, Laura Fry, William P. McDonald, and Kataro Shirayamadani in the next few years. In 1885, Mr. Nichols died, and the following year his widow remarried. She retired in 1890, leaving the firm under the directorship of William Watts Taylor, but she retained her own studio at the firm where she continued to experiment and create new works. In 1900 she produced an ovoid vase with seahorses (41). Its mount was probably made by E. H. Asano, a Japanese metalworker whom Shirayamadani had brought back to Rookwood with him when he returned from a trip to his homeland in 1894. The popularity at the time of Gorham's silver overlay technique encouraged Taylor to apply it to Rookwood's ceramics. Asano was retained to develop the process for vases, lamp bases, and so on.

Matthew Andrew Daly (1860–1937) joined Rookwood in 1882, after working briefly at the Matt Morgan Art Pottery. Born in Cincinnati, Daly attended the Cincinnati Art Academy. He was industrious and talented

41 Vase, decorated by Maria Longworth Nichols Storer, Rookwood Pottery Company (c.1900).
Ceramics and silvered metal. Decorated with 3 molded seahorses and an irregularly applied metallic luster glaze; the electroplated base is cast in full relief with an octopus, its tentacles entwined in the rope which rises from waves and sea-grass to support the vase. The creature's eyes are inset with tiger's eye cabochons. The base is inset with 2 freshwater pearls and 3 semicircular semiprecious jewels. 15½in. (39.4cm.) high.
Collection of the Charles Hosmer Morse Museum of American Art, Winter Park, Florida. Photo Theodore Flagg

and was to become one of Rookwood's highest paid decorators, remaining with the firm until 1903, when he joined the U.S. Playing Card Company as head of its art department.

Daly is credited with the development of Rookwood's "Limoges" form of underglaze decoration, but today his most important contribution to the firm's output is considered to be his Indian portraiture. His portrait vase of a proud Apache (42) captured with great power the defiance and suffering of the American Indian and helped promote public awareness of and sympathy for the Indians' plight. Rookwood introduced portraits into its repertoire around 1897. Included were not only Indians but also historical figures and actors, applied in the firm's standard glaze. The Indian portraits were copied mainly from photographs in contemporary books, such as *Indians of Today*, by George Bird Grinnell (1900), and *North American Indians*, by Edward S. Curtis (1907). In 1898, Frank Rinehart's photographs in the Trans-Mississippi International Exposition in Omaha contributed similarly to the public's awareness.

The vase's "standard" glaze became the firm's most readily identifiable hallmark, hence its name. Introduced in 1884, it is distinguished by its background of muted tones, usually chocolate or chestnut browns, ocher yellows, willow greens, and cherry reds, which blend into each other as the vase is turned. Kiln burns, which changed part of the brown background to a blackish color, were common. These colors provided the ground for sprays of flowers, cereals, or portraits which were applied in slip clay in warm complementary colors. A high gloss overglaze was then applied. This frequently had a yellow cast to provide the underneath decoration with a golden hue. The clay used on standard glaze wares was quarried mostly in the Ohio valley. Its natural color inclined the finished decoration towards the yellow-brown range of the spectrum.

The standard glaze remained Rookwood's principal form of decoration through the 1890s. It is seen again in Daly's vase portrait of a Samurai (43). The costume and posture were taken from photographs in reference books to which Rookwood subscribed and from periodicals such as Samuel Bing's *Artistic Japan*. The crisply modeled slip decoration, particularly in the linear folds of the warrior's robes, shows a quality of execution well above that of the average Rookwood commercial piece.

The *Japonisme* mania that swept America in the 1880s had a profound impact on Rookwood's ceramic decoration. Encouraged by Maria Longworth Nichols, the firm's decorators studied Japanese wares – pottery, scrolls, screens, bronzes, lacquerware, and textiles – in local private collections and at the Cincinnati Art Museum. Borrowed from Japanese art was an emphasis on nature, in particular the botanical realm. Nature quickly established itself as the firm's formal decorative vernacular. This vase (43) provides a rare depiction of traditional Japanese society.

The style of Kataro Shirayamadani (1865–1948) was, predictably, Oriental. He was born in Kanazawa, the home of Japanese Kutani ware. In 1887, while a member of the Deakin Bros traveling "Japanese Village" at the 13th Cincinnati Industrial Exposition, he accepted a position as a decorator at the Rookwood Pottery, its first non-American member of staff. In 1893 the firm sent him to his homeland to study local glazing techniques,

42 *Vase, decorated by Matthew Andrew Daly for the Rookwood Pottery Company (1899).*
Ceramics with a bronze collar. A baluster-shaped vase, decorated on the obverse with a bust of a brave of the Maricopa Apache tribe, in beige, tan, and brown tones on a standard high-glaze shaded brown ground. The shoulder is incised with a band of 5 stylized basketry motifs. 18⅛in. (46cm.) high; 5⅝in. (14.3cm.) diameter of mouth.
Ruth and Seymour Geringer

43 *Vase, decorated by Matthew Andrew Daly for the Rookwood Pottery Company (1889).*
Ceramics. A jar-formed vase, the obverse decorated in slip clay with a Ronin Samurai warrior, in tones of yellow, pink, brown, and black, on a shaded standard glaze ground. 13¼in. (33.6cm.) high; 5⁹/₁₆in. (14.1cm.) diameter of foot.
Collection of Fer-Duc, Inc., Newburgh, New York

Below left

44   Vase, decorated by Kataro
Shirayamadani, for the Rookwood Pottery
Company (1899).
*Ceramics. An ovoid vase, decorated at the
shoulder with 5 storks among cattails, in
green, brown, gray, and beige slip-applied
underglazes, on a black Iris glaze background.
14⅞in. (37.8cm.) high; 4⁵⁄₁₆in. (11cm.)
diameter of base.*
Private Collection

Below right

45   Vase, decorated by William Purcell
McDonald for the Rookwood Pottery
Company (1897).
*Ceramics. An ovoid vase, decorated with an
aquamarine panorama of 3 fish among sea-
grass beneath cresting waves, 3 seagulls on the
reverse. The image is modeled in underglaze
slip relief in white and pale green on a high
gloss sea-green glaze ground. 14⁹⁄₁₆in. (37cm.)
high; 6½in. (16.5cm.) diameter of mouth.*
Collection of William and Marcia Goodman

and while there he presented several examples of Rookwood pottery to the Emperor.

Shirayamadani was one of Rookwood's longest-serving and most gifted decorators, generating numerous awards for the firm at expositions. Some of his favorite themes, such as carp, wading birds, and flowers – particularly the chrysanthemum and peony – are shown in his 1899 vase (44).

The vase was included in the Rookwood exhibit at the 1900 Exposition in Paris. Marshall Fry, Jr., in his review of the exposition, wrote, "One large jar with flying storks and cattails against a black background is a masterpiece. The quality of the white of the birds and the treatment of edges is almost Whistleresque and I feel sure that this great master himself could find much to admire in this collection."[2] The vase also provides a prime example of Rookwood's Iris glaze, introduced in 1893/94. This glaze differed from the firm's "standard" brown glaze by the introduction of pastel hues, especially soft grays and blues, to replace the traditional brown as a background color. Both were high gloss glazes painted with slip decoration, but the Iris glaze was found to complement certain flowers better than the darker brown. Its light, fresh look proved to be an appealing alternative to the warm, but somber, hues of the standard brown. The public responded enthusiastically. By 1900 more varied, and stronger, contrasts between the primary images – flowers, birds, and so on – and their backgrounds were in evidence.

The black ground on Shirayamadani's vase (44) was the most dramatic, and rare, of the Iris glazes; a charcoal gray, or shaded gray-green-pink ground was more common. The glaze's most frequent exponent was Albert Robert Valentien. "I cannot say too much in favor of this type of Rookwood," he declared, "it being one of my favorites, especially where we were compelled to use flowers for decoration. In it I felt that I could express all the quality of tenderness that the real flower contained, perhaps even more fully than on paper or canvas, as the soft tones of the clays were well adapted to and lent themselves readily to this end."[3] In general, a limited repertory of flora – in white, yellow, and lavender – were used as decoration on Iris wares.

In 1894, at roughly the same time that it introduced its Iris glaze, Rookwood also produced its sea-green glaze. This, too, provided a welcome alternative to the firm's standard dark brown glaze, and its range of color – from warm greens to limpid, opaque blue-greens – was particularly suited to underwater themes, including fish and aquatic plants. The glaze evoked the changing colors and moods of the ocean, usually with the primary images in lighter colors.

After a slow start, the output of sea-green glazed wares increased steadily towards 1900, and most decorators included it in their repertoire. W.P. McDonald's vase of 1897 (45) provides an excellent example. McDonald (1865–1931) was born in Cincinnati and graduated from the School of Design at the city's university. He spent his entire 49-year career at Rookwood. This vase was created three years after he was appointed head of the firm's decorating room. A gifted and versatile decorator in the 1890s, McDonald transferred to Rookwood's Architectural Faience department in 1904. The architectural plaque (47), which he decorated with John D. Wareham, preceded the official opening of the department by two years,

46 Vase, decorated by Jens Jensen for the
Rookwood Pottery Company (1939).
Ceramics. A baluster-shaped vase, decorated
in an abstract style with 4 nude bathers and a
sheep in a floral landscape, in mottled white,
reddish-brown, gray, blue, and black high
glazes. 15⅝in. (39.7cm.) high; 4⅜in.
(11.1cm.) diameter of foot.
Dillenberg-Espinar Collection

47 Architectural Plaque, decorated by
William Purcell McDonald and John D.
Wareham for the Rookwood Pottery
Company (1901).
Faience. The plaque is modeled in bas-relief
with the Witches' scene from "Macbeth."
38in. (96.5cm.) high; 26½in. (67.3cm.) wide.
Private Collection

indicating that it was a unique commission, perhaps for a Shakespearean playhouse or theater director. Its incorporation of relief modeling and attention to detailing provide a rare example of what the firm could achieve in sculpted ornamentation. The lustered glaze appears to have been applied with an atomizer. Its workmanship is far more ambitious than the standard Vellum-glazed example produced by Rookwood, and also varies considerably in quality from the average item produced by the Architectural Faience department, which specialized in large volume decorative tiles and mantelpieces for the home, garden urns, statuary, and plaques such as those for the New York City subway system. The department remained in operation from 1903 until the late 1940s, its commercial success saving the firm repeatedly from insolvency, particularly between 1907 and 1913.

By 1939, however, even the Architectural Faience Department was not enough to save Rookwood from bankruptcy. As Herbert Peck noted,

During the period from 1935 to 1940, the pottery was kept open for business even though the office and salesrooms were manned by a skeleton staff. The "Visitors' Register" continued to be filled as people rode the historic incline railway to Mt. Adams and stopped at the pottery, where they made an occasional inexpensive purchase. In the decorating department, a few artists continued to work without regular pay, knowing that if and when money came in from sales they would get a share.[4]

The firm's financial reverses provided its individual decorators with time in which to pursue new technical and artistic avenues, and perhaps the vase by Jens Jensen, of 1939 (46), was designed in the spirit of experiment rather than for commercial reasons. Jensen arrived from Denmark in 1927 and joined Rookwood the following year. He was to remain with the firm until 1948. Jensen's style was characteristically the most progressive of his generation at Rookwood, described by some as "modernistic." A critic for the *Cincinnati Enquirer* defined it as "a bold, primitive style with a lot of imagination and feeling for his clay material – much of which he finishes in the manner of the European artists."[5] The vase illustrated here provides an example of his knowledge of earlier avant-garde European styles. Its expressionist imagery and soft naturalistic colors evoke the pre-World War I works of Matisse and Picasso, a style which had likewise inspired the Bordeaux potter, René Buthaud, from the mid-1920s.

Artus Van Briggle

Jensen was one of Rookwood's more original designers in the firm's later years. One of the stars of its early period was Artus Van Briggle, who, in his thirteen years with the pottery, produced some of the firm's most extraordinary and uncharacteristic wares.

Van Briggle (1869–1904) was born in Felicity, Ohio,[6] and at the age of seventeen entered the Cincinnati Academy of Art. To subsidize his studies, he took a job as a decorator at the Avon Pottery in 1886 and the following year transferred to Rookwood. His artistic style in his initial years at Rookwood was virtually indistinguishable from those of his colleagues: most of his pieces incorporate typical floral underglaze decoration on the firm's standard brown ground. He continued in his spare time to paint on

48 *"Lorelei" Vase, designed by Artus Van Briggle at the Rookwood Pottery Company (1897–98).*
Ceramics. A baluster-shaped vase, modeled in high relief with a figure of a nymph encircling the mouth, her spiraling body enveloped with trailing foliage. The mat sky-blue glaze is heightened with purple at the mouth. 9½in. (24.1cm.) high.
Private Collection

49 *"The Toast Cup," designed and modeled by Artus Van Briggle, Colorado Springs (1901).*
Ceramics. In the form of a chalice, modeled in high relief with a mermaid reaching for 2 fish among swirling waves, in a shaded pale and emerald mat green glaze. 11in. (28cm.) high; 7in. (17.8cm.) diameter.
Private Collection

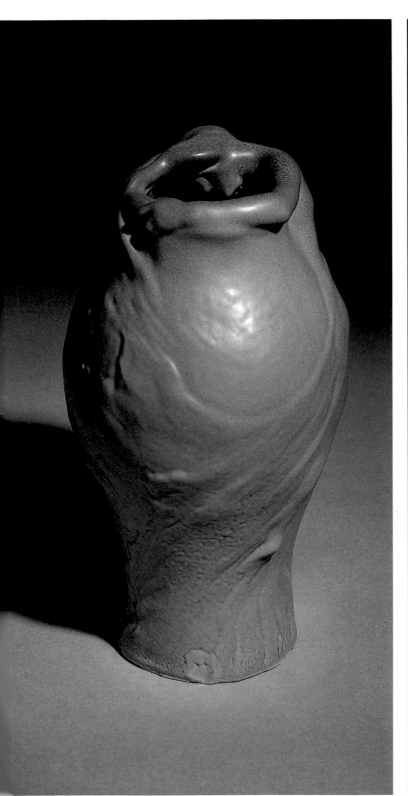

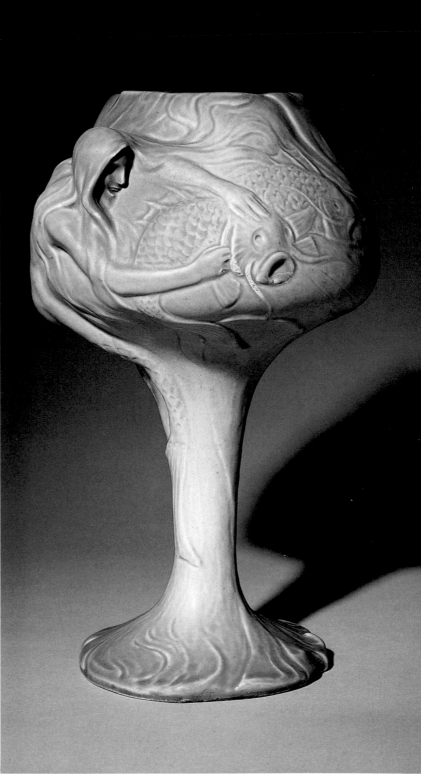

canvas, and when a painting of his was selected for display at the Columbian Exposition, Mrs. Storer granted him a scholarship to study at the Académie Julian and the Académie des Beaux-Arts in Paris for two years, a stay which was extended by a further twelve months. In 1896 he returned to Cincinnati, where he resumed his job at Rookwood as a pottery decorator. His spare time was taken up increasingly with glaze experimentation, including an attempt to rediscover the secret of the Ming dynasty's "dead" or mat glazes, which he applied in part to Art Nouveau-inspired vases.

Van Briggle had been exposed to the burgeoning Art Nouveau movement while he was in Paris and on his return he created the "Lorelei" vase (48).[7] The theme comes from the German folklore tale of the Lorelei Rock, created around 1800 by Clemens Brentano in his novel *Godwin*, a legend that underwent a revival in popularity in the 1890s, inspiring songs and dramatic sketches. Van Briggle's interpretation is seen today, however, as pure Art Nouveau. The recumbent maiden, with flowing tresses, is a *belle epoque* archetype.

The "Lorelei" vase was an extraordinary work to come from a Rookwood decorator: its dependence on modeling and its monochromatic glaze are atypical of the firm's standard commercial wares at the time, which employed a painterly decorating technique. A critic for *Brush and Pencil* noted that Van Briggle's relief modeling was usually extraneous to the vase, not part of it, and, in an obvious reference to the Lorelei model, added,

On a slender vase he will model the figure of a woman: her arms are clasped around the rim and she is gazing into the depths of it – a splendid conception, the working out of which none but a master would dare to undertake, for if unskillfully done the figure will be extraneous and so make the effort a failure. But Mr. Van Briggle makes the two one. Remove the figure of the woman, and there is no longer a vase, for her arms and head form the rim; her body, her hair, her drapery, make up the contour. With the most perfect feeling for form, he sees to it that the angles of her arms balance, that there is no salient point on one side of the vase without its complement on the other. The sweep of her hair balances the folds of her drapery; every line contributes to and preserves the harmony. Yet nowhere does this fine adjustment interfere one iota with the verisimilitude of the figure and pose, for then all would be lost.[8]

Van Briggle drew his inspiration for modeling from his sojourn in Paris; the relief motifs in his vases recall many similar models created by *fin-de-siècle* French sculptors such as Joseph Chéret, Charles Korschann, and Auguste Ledru. Most of these were in bronze. Very little of this aspect of the Art Nouveau movement was re-created by American craftsmen, and practically none of it in pottery, which explains in part the fresh impact which this imagery had on the American public when it was introduced by Van Briggle.

Van Briggle was forced to leave Ohio, and therefore Rookwood, due to ill-health. He resigned in March 1899 and moved to Colorado Springs, where he set himself up initially in the Colorado College, experimenting with local clays and glazes. In August 1901, he fired his first pieces at the Van Briggle Pottery at 615 North Nevada Avenue. In the same year his "Despondency" vase, a companion piece to the "Lorelei" which depicts a

50 *Vase, designed and modeled by Artus Van Briggle, Colorado Springs (c.1902). Ceramics. Of tapering cylindrical form, decorated with a band of conventionalized broad leaves on tall curved stems in a shaded mat dark green glaze. 15in. (38.1cm.) high. Private Collection*

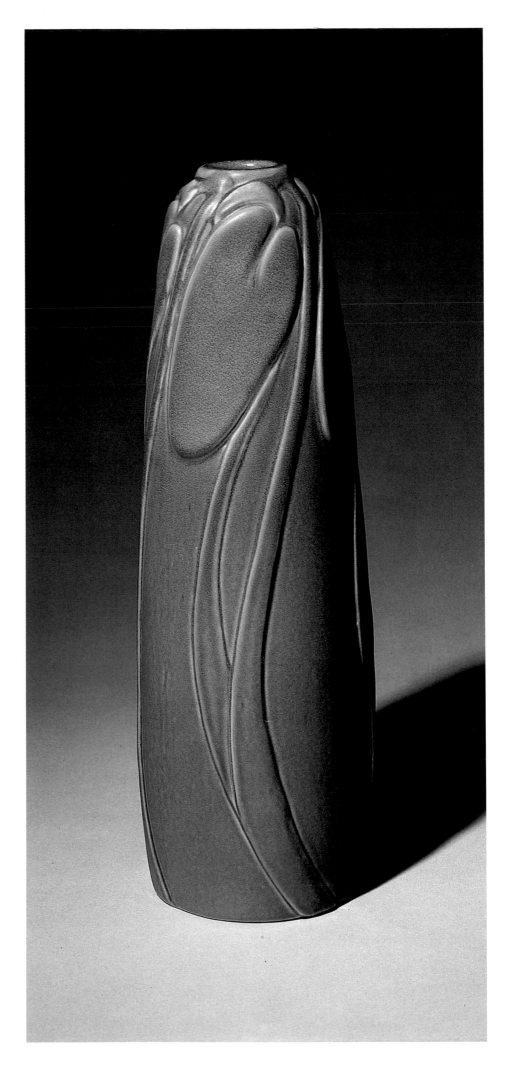

male nude similarly positioned at the mouth of the vase, was exhibited at one of the Paris Salons, and was purchased by the Louvre for an unprecedented $3,000.[9]

One of Van Briggle's earliest creations in Colorado (1901) was "The Toast Cup" (49). One other example of this piece is known, and it is possible that it was reproduced in a limited edition. The unglazed example illustrated in *Brush and Pencil* in 1901 appears to be slightly different in its detailing from the glazed one shown here, a difference which the subsequent application of Van Briggle's thick glaze would normally explain.[10] Although the model was illustrated frequently in contemporary articles on Van Briggle, both its inspiration and intended use remain unrecorded. Like the artist's "Lorelei" vase, the Toast Cup takes its theme from the French Art Nouveau movement, in particular the small bronze *objets d'art* which flooded the Paris Salons at the turn of the century. The mermaid was a variant on the nymph, naiad, and siren, which by 1905 became hackneyed in their country of origin.

While on his sabbatical in Paris, Van Briggle had been exposed to the Oriental collections at the Musée des Arts Décoratifs and Sèvres and had been particularly struck by the Chinese "dead" glazes, which he set out to emulate in his extracurricular pottery classes at the Académie des Beaux-Arts. A contemporary critic noted his progress,

As a result of much examination and thought, he reached the conclusion that in principle the modern highly vitrified and bright glazes were inartistic and that, through experiment, a partial return at least might be made to the soft dull surfaces of early Oriental fictiles, to reproduce which would be to restore a lost art. The specimens bearing the glaze so admired by Mr. Van Briggle belong to a remote epoch whose limits can not be fixed with precision. They include those pieces coated with the enamel more or less opaque, known to connoisseurs as *celadon*, which varies from reddish gray to a sea green ranging from dark to light, and a dull blue of great charm.[11]

The mat dark green on the vase of around 1902 illustrated here (50) falls into this category, its surface texture defined broadly as velvet-like and restful.

Van Briggle was not the first of his contemporaries to pursue the elusive mat glaze of ancient China; he was preceded by a host of French ceramicists, including Delaherche, Chaplet, and Bigot. He could not even claim a clear precedence in America as his experiments coincided with those of William Grueby of Boston, who had turned his energies to the same goal after the 1893 Columbian Exposition. Notwithstanding, Van Briggle's unrelenting pursuit of his desired glaze won the respect of the critics, who heaped praise on him. The vases were made in molds, each being dried, then biscuit-fired, glazed, and refired. The glaze was applied with an atomizer, which was operated with compressed air,

Like a cloud at sunrise the spray issues, and in this iridescent vapor the vase is bathed. Another color is often added to the first applied, or by holding the article at an angle to the spray one color is vignetted into another in exquisite blending; and if afterwards it be desired that certain lines be accentuated with darker or lighter tones the glaze is rubbed off in those places and the desired color put in with a brush, but always employing the glaze itself, for in this ware no paint is used. [12]

Like most of his models, this vase (50) has a strong Art Nouveau influence in its choice of a plant for its ornamentation. Other motifs adapted by Van Briggle after he moved to Colorado included the State's indigenous flora: spiderwort, mariposa, primrose, larkspur, and bowknot.

Late in 1902, Van Briggle sent a batch of pottery East, where it received almost unanimous acclaim in exhibits at the Craftsman Building in Syracuse, the Salon of the Société des Artistes Décorateurs in Paris, and, in the summer of 1904, at the Louisiana Purchase International Exposition. The triumph was shortlived, however; Van Briggle died in 1904. His widow and long-standing pottery partner, Anne Gregory Lawrence, continued to produce editions of his models with his small staff of assistants. Many of their wares, in the firm's characteristic dead glazes, continued to generate enthusiastic reviews from the critics.

Newcomb College Pottery

The 1904 Louisiana Purchase International Exposition also included work from the Newcomb College Pottery, New Orleans. Leona Fischer Nicholson's vase of 1902 (51) incorporates several elements from Newcomb's most popular wares of the 1900–10 period: the use of a white clay; a high gloss blue overglaze; the selection of the local environment as its decorative theme; and the formalization of this theme by the use, in part, of incised lines to silhouette the images.

Nicholson joined the College's Normal Art Program in 1896–97.[13] Unlike most of the other decorators at Newcomb, she was permitted to work as an independent studio potter, developing her own shapes and glazes. She was listed as a Newcomb decorator from 1903 to 1908, and then intermittently until 1929. The theme on this vase captures the serenity and whimsy of Newcomb's finest wares, one which Nicholson portrayed with great sensitivity, covering all aspects of the Gulf Coast's lush vegetation – spiderworts, gardenias, jasmine, angels' trumpets, and dogwood.

Like virtually all of Newcomb's pottery, this vase was thrown by Joseph Fortune Meyer, who joined the College around 1896 and stayed until his retirement in 1927.[14] Born in Alsace, Meyer learned his trade from his father, before joining the New Orleans Art Pottery, the forerunner to the Newcomb Pottery. During his long stay at Newcomb, he shaped the pots for a long succession of artist-decorators, experimenting continuously with different clays and glaze formulae. As Mary Given Sheerer, the Pottery's founder, later noted, "He was like some of the old-time cooks...who seasoned to taste and scorned too careful measures; consequently, the glaze could not be repeated."[15] Around 1904, when his eyesight began to fail, Meyer took on various assistants, including James Miller and his son Robert. He was succeeded in 1928 by Jonathan Browne Hunt.

It was in Meyer's last years with Newcomb that he threw the Anna Frances Simpson vase (52) of 1926 whose theme is among Newcomb's most popular and readily identifiable. Its panorama of Louisiana Live Oaks, cloaked in Spanish moss and early morning mist, evokes a nostalgic South. Henrietta Bailey, Sadie Irvine, and Corinne Chalaron also recreated this imagery on their vases, varying its effect with cypress, pine, and palm trees.

51   *Vase, decorated by Leona Fischer Nicholson, thrown by Joseph Fortune Meyer, for the Newcomb College Pottery (1902). White clay. A baluster-shaped vase with a collared rim, decorated with a frieze of trees in a high gloss blue glaze with a pale blue underglaze, the cream ground lightly streaked with blue, the trees silhouetted with incised lines. 12¹³/₁₆in. (32.5cm.) high; 5³/₈in. (13.7cm.) diameter.*
Dillenberg-Espinar Collection

52   *Vase, decorated by Anna Frances Simpson, thrown by Joseph Fortune Meyer, for the Newcomb College Pottery (1926). White clay. A baluster-shaped vase, modeled in low relief with a moonlit scene of moss-laden oak trees within a landscape, in mat bluish-green glaze. 13½in. (34.1cm.) high; 4⁵/₁₆in. (11cm.) diameter.*
Private Collection

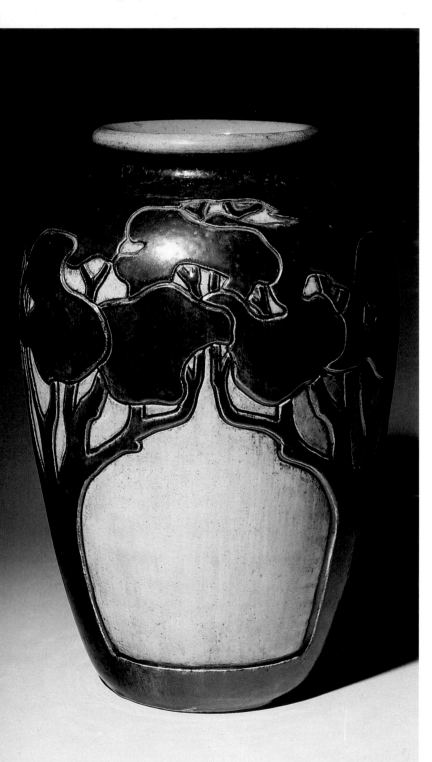

In the early 1930s, when an attempt was made to introduce "modern" designs, there was outcry from the College's clients, who demanded "the oak trees which are so typical of Louisiana.... Even now our agents all over the country are fighting the change."[16]

Newcomb introduced its semi-opaque mat glaze around 1911, to reduce its reliance on its high gloss blue and green overglazes of the previous decade. The muted blue-green palette of the mat glaze was admirably suited to the naturalistic themes introduced in the same period, providing the subdued effect achieved on this vase.

Simpson enrolled in the College's Normal Art program in 1902 and subsequently joined the ranks of the College's Art Craftsmen, exhibiting her pottery and embroidery intermittently until 1929.[17] A masterful decorator, she is credited with the Newcomb "Espanol" motif, a design based on an early Spanish mantelpiece form of decoration in the New Orleans French quarter.[18] She died in 1930.

The Grueby Faience Company

The Grueby Faience Company, the Gates Potteries, and the Fulper Pottery Company all put enormous inventiveness and effort around the turn of the century into the development of new glazes.

The mat green glaze developed by William H. Grueby (1867–1925), founder of the Grueby Faience Company, was received with some rhapsody by the *Boston Sunday Globe* in March 1901:

There is nothing just like this finish in any of the known examples of pottery, either modern or ancient. Its smoothness is the smoothness of the fresh watermelon peel, and its color is a suggestion of the deepest green of a very dark melon, without the stripes of light coloring. It is in this finish that the secret of the success of the Grueby pottery as a work of ceramic art lies. Mr. Grueby has a secret process by which the finish is made. The finish is not a glaze, such as one sees on common varieties of pottery; it is enamel, heavy and opaque, yet with a texture softer than the down of a rose petal and as enduring as jade or jasper.

Only in old Korean ceramics could a parallel be found. In 1900, the glaze's popularity was established internationally at the Exposition Universelle in Paris, where it was awarded two gold medals and one silver medal.

The glaze, shown on a double gourd vase (53) of around 1900 probably designed by George Prentiss Kendrick, had been refined by Grueby between 1893 (the date of the Columbian Exposition in Chicago) and 1897 (the year of incorporation of the Grueby Faience Company). It was to become the firm's hallmark. Its appeal lay both in the rich monotone of its coloring and its velvety, yet glossless, surface, qualities considered at the time unique to American pottery. Until then, dull finishes had usually been obtained either by sandblasting or by the immersion of the piece in an acid-bath.

The patterning on some green pieces, where the uneven application of the glaze has resulted in paler green veining, or splotches, which show at random through the surface layer, has led to the coinage "watermelon rind," referred to above, or "cucumber." Although Grueby introduced a range of other colors – for example, blue, yellow, ocher, brown, plum, and mustard – none was considered comparable to the mat green variety. This, the critics felt, captured precisely the quiet mood sought in Arts and Crafts interiors, particularly those of Gustav Stickley, who incorporated Grueby vases into many of his Craftsman room settings.

The leaf motif on this vase is typical of floral decorations used by Kendrick on many of the firm's wares. Most are flora indigenous to New England rendered in a sufficiently naturalistic manner to invite identification; for example, mullein, plantain, arrowhead, jonquil, water-lily, and lotus. Occasionally, a more abstract, or conventionalized, effect was provided, echoing Egyptian floral motifs from the Pharaonic period. In most instances, as on this vase, a vigorous technique of modeling made the leaves appear to stand out in full relief from the piece.

Kendrick was the firm's chief designer. In the early years (around 1898–99) his designs were thrown on the wheel and then modeled, for the most part, by young women graduates drawn from institutions in the Boston area, especially the Boston Art Museum School, the Massachusetts Normal School, and the Cowles Art School.[19] For the modeling process, the girls rolled clay into thin strands which were applied to the body of the vase.

There are roughly eight known examples of Kendrick's vase of around 1898–1902 (54). They vary slightly in their execution, especially in the detailing applied to the band of leaves on the shoulder; on some examples the incised lines are absent. These discrepancies underline the fact that Grueby pottery was entirely hand-made,[20] something in which the firm took justifiable pride, but which pushed its prices above those of competitors.

This model, more than most, shows the influence on Grueby's designs of the late nineteenth-century French potters, in particular Auguste Delaherche and Ernest Chaplet. Grueby was impressed by the French exhibit at the 1893 Columbian Exposition in Chicago, especially the works of Delaherche, which were

modeled with abstract leaf shapes, and these became the prototype for his own production.... At a point presumably before 1898 Grueby wrote to Delaherche and asked to buy samples of the French potter's work. Delaherche replied in a letter accompanied by quick sketches of some of his vases. This negotiation came to nought, however, because Grueby felt the prices were too high. Yet even without the French models, the memory of them was evidently strong enough to have an effect. The company's indebtedness to Delaherche was never hidden; to the contrary, they made "cheerful acknowledgment" of it at all times as though this enhanced their own product.[21]

Delaherche's influence is especially evident in this 7-handled vase, which took its form directly from a buttressed model by the Frenchman illustrated in *The Studio* in 1898.[22] The manner in which the handles extend outwards at their lower terminals is virtually identical. The model's broad mouth allowed it to be used as a vase and as a base in which to house the fuel canister on a kerosene table lamp.

The application of a second color to Grueby pottery was mostly limited to models with floral decoration. Even then, it was used selectively, as the critic Walter Ellsworth Gray noted in 1901,

Occasionally, it is true, a second color is used on some of the raised portions of the design, but when this is the case, the second color is only sparingly used, and the

Below left

53 Vase, probably designed by George
Prentiss Kendrick for the Grueby Faience
Company (c.1900).
Ceramics. Of double gourd form, decorated
with two bands of broad leaves in a mat dark
green glaze. 15½in. (39.4cm.) high; 7in.
(17.8cm.) diameter.
Private Collection

Below right

54 Vase, designed by George Prentiss
Kendrick for the Grueby Faience Company
(1898–1902).
Ceramics. The bands of 7 leaves on the body
and shoulder are intersected by 7 openwork
"buttress" handles. Decorated in a mat green
glaze. 10¹³⁄₁₆in. (27.5cm.) high; 4in. (10.2cm.)
diameter of mouth; 5¾in. (14.6cm.) diameter
of foot.
The Kay Collection

strictest care is taken to make it harmonize with the prevailing color of the entire piece. In a word, such decorative treatment as is resorted to serves merely to accentuate or in a sense outline the color of the body.[23]

In Ruth Erikson's vase with daisy decoration of 1905 (78), a second, and even a third, color has been used. Erikson was one of the women graduates employed by the Grueby Company to execute its designs. Her monogram on this vase shows the firm's attempt to emphasize the artistic value of its wares, though its application is virtually meaningless in a creative context, as the modeler's role was limited to the faithful reproduction of a given design. Only very narrow degrees of variance could be allowed, as part of the firm's business was generated by mail order catalogues, which included an illustration, with specifications, of each object. Uniformity was therefore essential.

The floral design on this vase shows clearly that Grueby's artistic philosophy at the turn of the century was more closely aligned with the Arts and Crafts Movement than with Art Nouveau. The firm avoided the most typical characteristics of European Art Nouveau, such as attenuated organisms and whiplash curves, in preference to a more restrained, and formal, representation of nature. A French potter would have depicted the daisies on this vase in a more fanciful, if not vigorous, and stylistic manner. Three other examples of this model are known.[24]

In addition to the vases for which it is famous, Grueby also undertook a wide range of secular and ecclesiastical tilework. Indeed, had it limited itself from the start to this type of architectural commission, it might have escaped the financial difficulties which beset it after 1900.

In the firm's earliest years, from 1892, when Grueby formed a short-lived partnership with Eugene R. Atwood, to 1897, tile commissions were in most part historically inspired. The firm frequently yielded to an eclectic range of styles suggested by the customer, in particular, an Italian Renaissance revivalism which included copies of Luca and Andrea della Robbia's ceramic relief panels.[25] From 1897, however, when Kendrick became chief designer, tilework took on a distinct character of its own, both in the use of the celebrated new Grueby mat glaze, and in the adoption of a style which resembled the flat two-dimensional poster art fashionable among Art Nouveau graphic artists in France and Belgium at the time. The design was formed by dividing the tile's surface into a series of recessed *champs* (fields) or *cloisons* (cells), into which the monochromatic glazes were poured, in the manner of medieval enamelware, before being fired. The protruding cell walls remained unglazed, providing the image with sharp linear definition.[26]

A fireplace surround (56) designed around 1902, probably by Addison Le Boutillier, was part of a large Grueby commission by Mr. T. W. Lawson for his home, "Dreamwold," in Cohasset, Massachusetts. Included were three faience fireplaces, bedroom and bathroom friezes, and miscellaneous tile-ware.[27] The house was demolished in the early 1980s. Other important Grueby domestic tilework commissions included a hearth exhibited at the 1905 Louisiana Purchase Exposition,[28] a bathroom for a Mrs. Searls in San Francisco, and a conservatory for a house in Montreal.[29] The fireplace

55   Vase, modeled by Ruth Erikson for the
Grueby Faience Company (1905).
Ceramics. With a band of 6 panels each with
4 yellow-centered white daisies on tall stems
among slender leaves, the flowers in bas-relief
on a mat green ground. 16½in. (41.9cm.)
high; 5in. (12.7cm.) diameter of mouth;
7¼in. (18.4cm.) diameter of foot.
Collection of the Charles Hosmer Morse
Museum of American Art, Winter Park,
Florida. Photo Theodore Flagg

56 *Fireplace Surround, probably designed*
by Addison Le Boutillier for the Grueby
Faience Company (c.1902).
Ceramics. Comprised of 7 tiles depicting a
farmer leading an ox wagon laden with
lumber along a country road. 60⅜in.
(154.3cm.) wide; 35¼in. (89.5cm.) high; 2in.
(5.1cm.) approximate thickness of the tiles.
Collection of William and Marcia Goodman

illustrated here provides a means of examining a wide range of the firm's glazes in juxtaposition: greens, blues, mauve, beige, and orange.

Le Boutillier's other designs included an eight-tile faience frieze, entitled "The Pines," showing a panorama of pine trees against distant hills.[30] The individual tiles appear frequently today as framed miniature landscapes. As with his predecessor Kendrick, Le Boutillier's designs are not identified on the finished piece. Only the initials of the modeler appear; for example, MK, MMR, EA, DC, or MR. This was consistent with the firm's policy of promoting the artistic merits of its wares.

The Fulper Pottery Company

The Fulper Pottery Company turned to the creation of art pottery around the turn of the century, at the same time as William Hill Fulper II began his experimentation with glazes. Fulper is credited with the invention in 1911 of the firm's "Famille Rose" glazes. Included were five distinct hues: "ashes of roses," "deep rose," "peach bloom," "old rose," and "true rose."[31] Fulper's discovery attained instant celebrity for the firm as the formula for the extinct Chinese *famille rose* glazes had eluded ceramicists since its discontinuation nearly two centuries earlier. Although potteries such as Royal Doulton in Staffordshire, England, had perfected a red *sang de boeuf* commercial glaze (also known as ox-blood or *rouge flambé*) no one had been able to create a glaze with the texture and subtle shading of the pink "Famille Rose." Partly due to the high costs incurred in its production (and the correspondingly high percentage of pieces damaged in the kiln), and also because it was considered sound marketing policy to limit production in order to promote exclusivity, the firm offered each of its "Famille Rose" models as unique, available by special order only: "The rarity of the glaze and the necessarily heavy expense in its production will keep this rose pottery in the curiosity class. The valuations run from $50 up."[32] Prices, such as the $125 for a vase of 1914 (57), sometimes amounted to ten times that of standard prices. To underline the importance of its "Famille Rose," the firm donated several pieces to museums, including three in 1911 to the Philadelphia Museum of Art, and two in 1915 to the Newark Museum.[33]

The notation on this 1914 vase, *taken from an old Japanese piece*, was only partially correct. Whereas its form evolved from nineteenth-century Japanese ceramics, these, in turn, had been inspired by Chinese ceramics of the K'ang-shi period (1662–1722). As a contemporary critic noted, "The shapes this company is producing in the 'Famille Rose' are modeled after the old Chinese shapes, or when possible are taken direct from the pieces themselves, when these are available."[34] Vessel shapes included beakers, temple jars, and globular bottles.

Examination of the glaze on this vase suggests, at first glance, that it was either applied unevenly, or that it has a translucency which allows the stoneware body to show through the glaze in places. It is more probable, however, that the irregular application of the glaze was caused by slight overfiring which burned away some of the original pink color.

A direct Chinese influence is found both in the shape and glaze of a baluster-shaped vase of around 1918–26 (58). It is one of the firm's line of

Below

57 Vase, executed at the Fulper Pottery
Company (1914).
Ceramics. A globular body and short flaring
neck and twin applied fin-shaped handles,
decorated in an irregular pink "Ashes of
Roses" glaze with traces of gray. 12⅛in.
(30.8cm.) high; 10in. (25.4cm.) diameter.
Collection of the Newark Museum, Newark,
New Jersey

Below left

58   Vase, Vase-Kraft no. 590, executed at
the Fulper Pottery Company (1918–26).
Ceramics. Baluster shaped, with a collared
rim, in a trailing black glaze shading to brown
on an apple green ground. 16¹⁵/₁₆in. (40.5cm.)
high; 5⅞in. (15cm.) diameter of mouth;
5⅛in. (13cm.) diameter of foot.
Dillenberg-Espinar Collection

Below right

59   Vase, Vase-Kraft no.592, executed at
the Fulper Pottery Company (1918–22).
Ceramics. In a copper-dust crystalline glaze,
the molded baluster body decorated with a
band of 6 formalized leaves beneath a reversed
band of leaves on the shoulder. 11⅛in.
(28.3cm.) high; 3⅞in. (9.8cm.) diameter of
mouth; 4¾in. (12.2cm.) diameter of foot.
Collection of David and Beth Cathers

Vase-Kraft models, introduced in 1909. The glaze provides the only ornamentation. Fulper's belief in the supremacy of glaze alone was inspired no doubt by the parallel movement at the turn of the century in Paris, led by potters such as Delaherche and Chaplet. Another likely influence was Charles F. Binns, formerly of the Royal Worcester Porcelain works in England, who in 1877 had been appointed director of the Trenton Technical School of Science and Art. The proximity of Trenton to Flemington suggests that Fulper and his staff would have been familiar with Binns's writings on glazes and his vociferous opposition to the technique of pictorial decoration in addresses to local pottery groups. Binns had a great admiration for Chinese ceramics, in which "the fire itself was the decoration." He wrote in *The Craftsman*,

The pride of the potter is that his clay shall yield to the furnace: flowing and mingling in matchless beauty and endless variety. But the glazes must also acknowledge the artistic restraint by which his whole work is controlled.... I endow either porcelain or pottery with brilliant color, pulsing with life and radiance, or with tender texture, soft and caressing: color and texture which owe their existence and their quality to the fire – this is art.[35]

This view matches precisely that of William Hill Fulper in his development of the firm's *flambé*, mirrored, and lustered glazes.

Crystalline glazes were among Fulper's proudest achievements, despite the fact that they were notoriously unpredictable. Reviewing the firm's exhibit at the 1915 Panama-Pacific Exposition, a critic noted, "Crystalline glazes are ceramic curios, only appreciated by those interested in the industry and only a few enthusiastic chemists have been able to produce a specimen."[36] For this reason, Fulper initially produced crystalline glazes for exhibition purposes only. The near impossibility of obtaining the correct effect – or, rather, one which could be reproduced at the level of consistency necessary for commercial purposes – held production to a minimum. The vagaries of the kiln and the random manner in which the crystal molecules multiplied led to unhappy experimentation instead of profits. Effects varied from isolated crystal formations resembling snowflakes or frost, to the firm's noted "leopard skin" glaze.

The copper dust variation, used in a Vase-Kraft model of around 1918 to 1922 (59) was extremely rare. It is valued for its finely granulated and even surface, and was used in combination with other Fulper glazes; for example, Chinese blue flambé, green flambé, and mirror black. Only three examples of this model are known.

Tiffany Studios

Louis Comfort Tiffany cloaked his early experimentation with pottery in some secrecy. His interest in the medium was probably first whetted by the works of vanguard French potters, which he would have seen during his visits in the mid-1890s both to the annual French Salons and to Samuel Bing's new Maison Art Nouveau, through which he exhibited a selection of windows from December 1895. In 1900, at the Exposition Universelle, he remained sufficiently impressed to invite a group of contemporary French potters – including Delaherche, Hoentschel, Dalpayrat, Bigot, Doat,

60 *"Salamander" Vase*, designed by Louis Comfort Tiffany, Tiffany Studios (1906–09). Ceramics. Designed as a cabbage with a profusion of flowers above the plant-form body, applied with 3 openwork stems, the foot molded with extending leaves, each with a salamander. In a streaked dark and pale green glaze. 9½in. (24.1cm.) high; 6½in. (16.5cm.) wide.
Private Collection

61 *"Jack-in-the-Pulpit" Vase*, designed by Louis Comfort Tiffany, Tiffany Studios (1906–09).
Bisque. Designed as a cluster of Jack-in-the-Pulpits with openwork stems at the neck, the flowers modeled in high relief above lower stems and leaves. 12in. (30.5cm.) high; 4½in. (11.4cm.) diameter.
Private Collection

Chaplet, and Jeannerey[37]–to exhibit the following year at Tiffany Studios.

During this time Tiffany had been quietly at work on his own ceramic research at the Corona factory. Early pieces from his Favrile Potteries were heavy and uninspired. But by around 1906 he was producing boldly sculpted pieces of an impressive lightness and vigor. Several Tiffany pottery pieces, such as his "Salamander" vase (60), the "Pussy Willow", and the "Corn Sheaf", were recreated from earlier *repoussé* enamel on copper models, though their muted earth tones set them apart esthetically from the vibrant hues of their enameled counterparts. Their three-dimensional organic forms recalled especially the Art Nouveau creations in the glass of Emile Gallé and his Ecole de Nancy colleagues some years earlier. The bold naturalism of his "Jack-in-the-Pulpit" vase (61) – a favorite Tiffany flower – also recalls Gallé. The openwork leafage at the top of this vase and the protruding petals are rare in Tiffany's work; he usually preferred a more stylized interpretation, achieved in ceramics by images molded in bas-relief. The high fragility of this model has added to its rarity.

A "Fern Frond" vase (62) of around 1906 shows the faithful way in which Tiffany interpreted nature, one at odds with the attenuations of the European Art Nouveau movement.[38] He embellished his pottery with common plants, grasses, and cereals; for example, milkweed, corn, toadstools, pussy willow, and artichokes.[39] The floral motifs either protrude in bas-relief from conventionally shaped vessels, or, in the bolder examples, the theme's sculpted three-dimensionality dominates the piece, obscuring its function.

Tiffany pottery was either thrown in the traditional manner on the wheel, or sculpted by hand from lumps or coils of damp clay. Finishing operations included the manual application of extra ornamentation, and carving and trimming to sharpen images. The piece was then molded in plaster, from which duplicates were cast. These, in turn, were again meticulously hand-finished and given an incised LCT monogram (with serial numbering, where appropriate) before being fired in a coal-burning kiln. Tiffany pottery was, therefore, mass produced, but editions appear to have been limited to ten examples, or thereabouts. In an Arts and Crafts context, this deviated from William Morris's philosophy concerning the individual work of art, even though the original piece was handmade, but it was consistent with Tiffany's goal of introducing a wide range of crafted items at affordable prices. Variety was afforded by the fact that some pieces were left unglazed, allowing the customer to select his own finish and color, which he could do through the aid of sample tiles.[40]

Glazes were mostly in complementary earth tones: ivory, beige, ocher, brown, and greens, the range of the palette narrower than that applied to the Studios' enamels and glassware, which were often brilliantly springlike in comparison to the autumnal tones of the ceramic pieces. Ivory and green were the most favored glazes, their light transparency allowing the white clay body to show at the points of highest relief. Some models were glazed only on the interior, the outside remaining in its original fired state which today, unfortunately, is often discolored through handling and wear.

Tiffany Studios continued to produce pottery wares until sometime between 1917 and 1920, at the approximate time that Tiffany himself

62 "Fern Frond" Vase, designed by Louis Comfort Tiffany, executed at Tiffany Furnaces (c.1906).
Cast and glazed semiporcelainous clay. With 7 scrolled openwork fronds joining at the top, each with incised relief detailing on an undecorated ground. 10⅞in. (27.7cm.) high; 11½in. (29.2cm.) diameter.
Collection of Cooper-Hewitt Museum, the Smithsonian Institution's National Museum of Design, New York. Gift of Marcia and William Goodman

withdrew from the firm's operation. It appears from his first biographer, De Kay, that Tiffany had tired of the medium sometime earlier, as he referred in *The Art Work of Louis C. Tiffany*, published in 1914, in the past tense to Tiffany's interest, "glazes on pottery claimed much of his time during certain years." The decline in quality becomes evident. Following the introduction in 1910 of "bronze pottery" – a technique in which a sleeve of bronze foil was applied to the pottery's outer surface and then patinated or given a gilt or silvered finish by electroplating – production became uninspired, even perfunctory. The vigor of the earlier pierced and sculpted models was absent, in its place a range of conventional shapes and monochromatic glazes. Today the bronze pottery technique, particularly, seems curiously inappropriate for a medium in which glaze is paramount.

Commercially, pottery appears to have been the least successful of Tiffany's ventures. The press compounded the problem by providing it with virtually no publicity at all. Almost the only contemporary reference to it was in the *Blue Book* published by Tiffany *&* Company, in which a list was provided of items offered at the Fifth Avenue store. Critics ignored it in their reviews of American pottery to the point where one suspects a conspiracy. The attitude seems to have been that with so many monumental achievements to his name in glass, windows, lamps, art glass, and so on, Tiffany's pottery would appear secondary both to himself and others. Today, the appreciation of the glazes and low relief modeling on Tiffany's pottery has established it as a favorite among American Arts and Crafts collectors, largely a different audience from that for Tiffany's glass and metalwares.

The Gates Potteries

Teco ware evolved as a byproduct of the American Terra Cotta *&* Ceramic Company (founded 1881), a manufacturer of architectural ceramic elements and tiles situated in the countryside at Terra Cotta, 45 miles northwest of Chicago.[41] The Gates Pottery was established as a subsidiary company in 1886. The firm's president, William Day Gates, a potter by profession, spent his leisure hours experimenting with clay, an avocation which led by 1902 to the formation of the firm's Teco line of art pottery (Gates derived the word "Teco" from the first syllables of the two words, Terra Cotta).[42]

At first, architect and artist friends contributed designs to those created by Gates. Several of Chicago's best-known architects, including Frank Lloyd Wright, William LeBaron Jenney and his partner, William B. Mundie, Hugh M. G. Garden, William J. Dodd, N. L. Clarke, and George N. Nimmons, submitted designs. Rejecting the historicism which had characterized American architecture throughout most of the nineteenth century, Wright and other members of the Prairie School developed architectonic forms for Gates which reflected their revolutionary building style. Simple, uncluttered shapes predominated. Handles became plain lugs or vertical struts that helped to accentuate the piece's architectonic form. Ornament, when included, consisted of geometric configurations or single abstract floral motifs, such as hollyhock, poppy, or sumac. Teco became the ceramic expression of the Prairie School, a fact appreciated again today by

collectors of Arts and Crafts pottery. In addition to vases, jardinières, hanging wall vases, and table lamp bases were produced.

Wright's known designs for Gates included a "triplicate" vase, 32in. high, which was priced at $30, among the highest in the firm's price lists. For Wright, Gates cast in terracotta the statuette, *Flower in a Crannied Wall*, and fountain, *The Moon Children*, both created by the sculptor Richard Bock in 1902 for the entrance of the Dana house in Springfield, Illinois. Also for the Dana house, Wright created a blue-green glazed vase (63). This may originally have contained a metal liner for use as a fern stand.

By 1911, when the firm had an established design department, roughly five hundred models had been put into production.[43] Pieces were molded, rather than thrown, to guarantee exact duplication and to minimize production costs.[44] Gates justified this departure from the Arts and Crafts handicraft philosophy pursued at Grueby and Newcomb by the fact that molding ensured, far more reliably than hand-throwing, the quality control essential for mass-produced items sold through magazine advertisements and sales catalogues. Any deviance from the form offered in an illustration could lead to the piece being returned as defective. A range of domestic wares, such as candlesticks, lamps, pitchers, and tea services, was offered. The potteries appear to have closed around 1923. The buildings were purchased in 1929 by George A. Berry, Jr., who renamed the company The American Terra Cotta Corporation.[45]

Although Gates invited a number of architects and artists to contribute designs for his Teco wares, at least half of the five hundred models put into production by 1911 were from his own designs. His style was diverse, including modern interpretations of Classical Greek and oriental shapes, conventionalized flora, and, as in a vase of around 1905 (64), a strong architectural influence. In its crisp symmetry, the vase expresses his philosophy of the union of line and form.

Like the Grueby Faience Company, the Gates Potteries placed special emphasis on the first glaze which it perfected, the mat green shown in a vase designed by Fritz Albert (65).[46] Although a wide range of other colors was introduced subsequently, between 1904 and 1911 – for example, brown, blue, red, yellow, platinum gray and, briefly, a selection of America's first crystalline glazes – the firm mainly promoted its distinctive mossy or velvety "Teco green," which it described as "a peculiarly pleasing shade, one that fits in and harmonizes with nearly all surroundings."[47] A team of qualified chemists, including two of Gates's sons, experimented continuously with glaze formulae, firing, and cooling, to eliminate color inconsistencies and accidental effects. Notwithstanding, it was necessary to include a disclaimer in Teco sales catalogues to pre-empt customer dissatisfaction: "It is not possible in burning pottery to maintain an exact tone in successive kilns … every piece of Teco is itself alone – though all are closely similar."

The vase's designer, Fritz Albert, was educated at the Royal Academy in Berlin and was commissioned by the German government to collaborate on the Electrical Building at the 1893 Columbian Exposition in Chicago, following which he continued his sculptural studies in Rome.[48] On returning to the U.S.A., he was hired by William Day Gates as a clay modeler and artist. Albert was deeply inspired by nature and his vase

Below left

64 Teco Vase, model no. 377, designed by
William Day Gates, the Gates Potteries
(c.1905).
*Ceramics. The flaring body has 4 buttress
supports and is decorated with a mat green
glaze. 12¹⁄₁₆in. (30.6cm.) high; 7³⁄₄in.
(19.7cm.) diameter of mouth; 8³⁄₄in.
(22.2cm.) diameter of foot.*
Collection of Joel Silver

Below right

65 Teco Vase, model no. 192, designed by
Fritz Albert at the Gates Potteries (1904–5).
*Ceramics. The baluster body is molded with
lightly ribbed spiraling leaves beneath an
applied band of 6 leaves spiraling in the
opposite direction; in a mat green glaze.
14³⁄₈in. (36.5cm.) high; 4¹⁄₄in. (10.8cm.)
diameter of mouth; 4⁷⁄₈in. (12.4cm.) diameter
of foot.*
Private Collection

designs were primarily floral, as were those of three other designers at the Gates Potteries: Hugh M.G. Garden, Fernand Moreau, and William J. Dodd.[49] Two outside designers retained by Gates, Blanche Ostertag, a young Chicago illustrator, and Orlando Giannini, a partner in the glass firm Giannini & Hilgart, pursued the same decorative style. In 1907, Albert left Gates to join the Northwestern Terra Cotta Company.

The complex reticulated leaf design on this vase required extra handwork as each leaf had first to be molded and then applied individually to the body of the base. For this reason this type of floral model was gradually phased out in favor of more pure, and architectural, pieces.

Unlike other potteries, which applied their glazes by brush or an immersion process, the Gates Potteries used the commercial airbrush technique it had developed for its architectural terracotta and brick wares. Susan Stuart Frackleton, a contemporary critic, described the process:

It [the vase] is then placed on a little revolving pedestal in front of a great, concave, metal disc, so arranged that the surplus glaze which is thrown against its surface will drain down into a receptacle and be preserved. To the biscuit the workman then applies the nozzle of a giant atomizer, which consists of two rubber tubes, one conveying liquid glaze, and the other compressed air. He then sprays the vase with an even coating of the glaze, revolving it slowly on its pedestal to suit his requirements.[50]

The considerable amount of coverage afforded Teco in contemporary magazines shows the esteem in which it was held at the time. In *House Beautiful* it was matched, in respective importance, with the handwrought pieces of Adelaide Alsop Robineau, by a critic who judged each "pre-eminent in its own line."[51] Today, the particular merits of Teco ceramics are sometimes overlooked, along with those of other potteries which employed a similar single-glaze type of decoration, such as Grueby, Hampshire, and Weller.

The Weller Pottery

Samuel A. Weller of the Weller Pottery, Zanesville, Ohio, began to experiment in pottery in 1872, but it was only in the early 1890s that he introduced a commercial range of wares.[52] He produced underglaze works in reds and browns, hand-decorated with fruit, flowers, and portraits in a process known as Louwelsa. From 1897, additional lines were added, including Dickens' Ware, Eocean, and Samantha. Business thrived until World War I, but then gradually declined. In 1947 the Essex Wire Corporation of Detroit purchased the controlling stock. Pottery production was discontinued the following year.

The distinct iridescent glaze of the "Sicardo" vase (66) was the product of Jacques Sicard, formerly an assistant chemist to Clément Massier in Golfe-Juan, France. Samuel Weller hired him around 1901,[53] and this vase was designed between then and 1907. Weller was aware of the popularity in Europe of Massier's metallic luster Art Nouveau ceramics, similar to the luster produced at the time by the Zsolnay pottery in Pecs, Hungary. Weller introduced "Sicardo" as part of a series of new wares developed to

66 "Sicardo" Vase, designed and executed by Jacques Sicard at the Weller Pottery (1901–7).
Ceramics. Baluster-shaped, molded in bas-relief with 4 iris sprays in a metallic rainbow glaze on a highly iridescent and mirrored maroon ground. 12^{15}/₁₆in. (33cm.) high; 4^{3}/₁₆in. (10.2cm.) diameter of base.
Dillenberg-Espinar Collection

compete with the other Zanesville potteries. On his arrival in Ohio, Sicard experimented for two years with metallic glazes. Accustomed to the use of peat or brushwood kilns in France, he rejected the natural gas models at the Weller Pottery, taking the brush from around Zanesville to fuel experiments. Soon a range of lusterware, in tones of pink, blue, bronze, purple, and maroon, was introduced. The vases were first treated with a metallic preparation and then decorated with conventional designs in chemically prepared pigments. The glaze was fired at a very high temperature, which transformed the pottery's surface into a kaleidoscope of iridescent colors. Sicard's success can be measured by the fact that it is often difficult to distinguish between his and Massier's works.

"Sicardo" or "Weller Sicardo" ware was produced with considerable commercial success until 1907, when Sicard returned to his native France. The firm continued to offer it until 1912 while inventory lasted. The iridescent glaze of "Sicardo" was so similar to the Tiffany Studios' glassware that Tiffany & Company offered the line exclusively at its New York Store. Sicard died in 1923.

The Middle Lane Pottery

In 1893, Theophilus Anthony Brouwer (1864–1932) moved from New York, where he had been studying at the New York College and the National Academy of Design, to East Hampton.[54] It was there that he began his experiments in glazed ceramics, opening a studio the following year. Brouwer's choice of pottery as his artistic discipline was extraordinary. He had exhibited canvases at the National Academy in New York, but he had no formal training in chemistry or the potter's craft. His technique evolved along unconventional lines, on a trial-and-error basis perfected through hours of labor and experiment.

Brouwer is best known for his Fire Painting technique, which was defined at the time as

The generic term given the new iridescent pottery which may be used to describe the ware literally. All of the strangely beautiful designs found upon the pots and vases are due to the action of the flames alone. No brush-work or hand-illumination whatsoever takes place. The artist had gained such mastery of his method that he is able to direct a general color scheme or decorative effect. It is a drab, uninteresting looking mixture, that glaze. But its potency in the hands of its inventor seems pure magic. With exactly the same glaze, applied in precisely the same manner, Mr. Brouwer is able to produce half a dozen different color schemes at the same firing. This seems incredible, but it has been witnessed too often to admit of doubt. Nor is this all of the wonder. If a finished iridescent piece is placed in an ordinary pottery kiln, and burned sufficiently hard, all of the coloring will disappear, leaving a plain white enamel, but Mr. Brouwer will take this piece, and by manipulating it in the fire as before will restore it to its pristine state, as beautifully opalescent as ever.[55]

Brouwer's firing technique was, therefore, totally at variance with tradition. He discarded the proven method of gradually heating the kiln and then allowing it to cool off thoroughly before withdrawing the piece, to prevent the possibility of cracking, and determined instead to utilize the vagaries of the kiln, rather than minimize them. The glazed pottery was

67   *Fire Painted Vase, designed and executed by Theophilus Anthony Brouwer at the Middle Lane Pottery (1898–1902). Ceramics. A baluster-shaped vase with flaring rim, decorated with a variegated high gloss brown, orange, yellow, and caramel drip glaze applied over an oily iridescent glaze shaded in metallic gold, red, plum, and maroon, the underside with central aperture. 12¾in. (32.3cm.) high; 4¼in. (10.8cm.) diameter of mouth.*
Collection of R. A. Ellison

exposed almost directly to the full heat of the open furnace, where it remained for as little as seventeen minutes while the glaze matured. It was then withdrawn with tongs and cooled at room temperature. The decorative effect came from the impact of the flames, which Brouwer had learned to anticipate and regulate to a fine degree.

Fire Painting was one of five processes developed by Brouwer around the same firing procedures. The others were defined as Iridescent Fire Painting, Sea Grass Fire Painting, Kid Surface, and Gold Leaf Underglaze. The vase illustrated here (67) is marked *FLAME*, which the artist claimed was a combination of the five, which he developed in East Hampton and perfected after his move to West Hampton in 1902. He considered his Flame pottery the culmination of his work, "each example being a carefully studied combination of form, color, and texture." Each piece was unique, capturing the prismatic hues and rainbow iridescence of the spectrum in its own inimitable way.

Brouwer's mastery of iridescent and lustered glazes evokes comparison with the Weller Pottery. He handled all aspects of his studio's production personally: the throwing, molding, decorating, and firing.

The Dedham Pottery

In his unorthodoxy, Brouwer has often been bracketed with Hugh Cornwall Robertson (1844–1908). Robertson's volcanic glaze, shown here in a baluster-shaped vase (68), provided him with a very personal form of expression; its lavish, organic appearance was unlike anything attempted by any of his contemporaries except Brouwer. No record has survived of exactly when he began to experiment with it, but the groundwork was no doubt laid in the late 1880s, after a period of obsessive experimentation to rediscover the Oriental *sang-de-boeuf* glaze. At the time he tried a wide range of glaze formulae in high-fire tests, some of which must have yielded positive results. Most extant pieces of volcanic ware are signed with the name of the Dedham Pottery, Dedham, Massachusetts, signifying that they were made between 1896 and 1908, the year of Robertson's death. An article in *House Beautiful* in 1897 pinpoints the date when the technique was introduced: either in that year or shortly earlier.

He [Robertson] has recently taken out some marvelous specimens of what might be called accidental glazes. The pieces may receive as many as ten or a dozen firings before they reach their final state. The glazes are put on the tops of the vases in a thick paste. Subjected to the intense heat of the furnace, the colors developing run down over the sides, as boiling sap runs down over the pot in a sugar camp. It is not wholly accident, by any means, for the potter's watchful eye notes the progressive stages of the melting point, and the mottled or striped or clouded effects are foreseen. It requires no little skill to proportion the amount of paste to the temperature so that the top shall not be left bare or thin, yet that sufficient shall cover the base. Sometimes the heat causes whole patches of the glaze to fly off, leaving the red surface of the body in too odious contrast. Then the vase is condemned and must be fired again.... In many of the firings the glaze actually boils on the surface of the vase, and if this boiling process is arrested at just the right moment, the pocked surface of the swelling sides, with its glittering combination of tints, is an added beauty.... No two are alike; the variety is amazing; there are such

68   *Volcanic Vase, designed and executed
by Hugh Cornwall Robertson at the Dedham
Pottery (1896–1908).
Stoneware. The beige body is applied with a
thick, irregular dark green glaze beneath a
bubbly greenish-white volcanic glaze which
extends downwards from the rim on both the
exterior and interior, with several slightly
open firing bubbles. 7⅛in. (18.1cm.) high;
3⁷⁄₁₆in. (8.8cm.) diameter of foot.
Collection of R. A. Ellison*

opalescent hues, such wonderful marriages of colors, such contrasts and blendings, such gradations and fluctuations. One recurs for figures again and again to that of the setting sun – stormy sunsets and serene sunsets.[56]

Robertson was a member of a remarkable dynasty of potters. James Robertson, his father, was an accomplished British potter, who had moved to the U.S.A. in 1853 with his wife, daughter, and three sons (George, Alexander, and Hugh).[57] They eventually settled in Massachusetts, where in 1860 the father organized the Plympton & Robertson Pottery Company in East Boston. In 1866 Alexander established his own pottery in the Chelsea marshes. Hugh joined him a year later, and in 1872 their father and George followed. They named their pottery the Chelsea Keramic Art Works.

The 1876 Centennial Exposition had a profound effect on Hugh, who marveled at the latest glaze creations from Europe, particularly Haviland's underglaze painted decoration. Even more influential was the selection of subtle masterpieces from the Orient. On his return to Chelsea, Hugh embarked on a period of concentrated experimentation. Changes were forthcoming, however: in 1878 George left; two years later their father died; and in 1884 Alexander set off for the West Coast. Hugh was left as the Chelsea master potter.

The years 1884–89 were arduous. He set himself the task of rediscovering the *sang-de-boeuf*, or Dragon's Blood, red glaze of China's Ming period. So obsessed did he become with his search that the pottery's commercial production plummeted and he developed lead poisoning, but by 1889 he had discovered an elusive ruby glaze which he alluded to sardonically as "Robertson's blood." Exhausted and penniless, at the height of his creative powers but unable even to pay for the fuel of his kiln, Robertson closed the pottery. In 1891 a group of wealthy Bostonians provided the finances to convert it into a viable business. The studio was moved to more modern facilities in East Dedham, ten miles southwest of Boston. The Dedham Pottery opened in 1896. Robertson, by now acclaimed nationally for his *sang-de-boeuf* and volcanic glazes, was incidental to the pottery's commercial production of ceramic crackle ware, a charming range of plates, cups, and bowls hand-painted with flora, domestic animals, and insects. The pottery was revitalized, receiving honors at the International Exposition in Paris (1900), and the St. Louis World's Fair (1904).

The Grand Feu Pottery

Cornelius Brauckman (1863–1951) was born in Missouri and moved to Los Angeles in around 1909, opening the Grand Feu Art Pottery in late 1912.[58] Three years later he was awarded a Gold Medal at the 1915 San Diego Exposition and in February 1916 was listed as a participant in Los Angeles's first Annual Arts and Crafts Salon. No further listing of the pottery is recorded after that year. Four vases in the Collection of the Smithsonian Institution, donated by the artist, bear testimony to the caliber of his workmanship.

Grand Feu pottery, as the name indicates, is the process of firing ceramics at a temperature sufficiently high to fuse the body and glaze simultaneously.

69 *Vase, designed and modeled by Cornelius Brauckman at the Grand Feu Art Pottery (1913–16).*
White stoneware. A baluster-shaped vase, with lobed quatrefoil lower half, decorated with irregular horizontal bands shading from light khaki, through orange and mottled brown to blue-black below, the lobes in beige. Collection of P. G. Pugsley & Sons Antiques, San Francisco, California. Photo Robert Reiter

This occurs at roughly 2500°F. One of the firm's brochures defined its product as *Grès-Cérame*, that is, white stoneware clay, a vitrified form of clay similar in its properties to porcelain, but lacking both its translucency and pure whiteness. Today, *Grès* is generally identified as stoneware.

Brauckman rejected both applied and painted decoration, relying on the natural, often fortuitous, interaction of the heat and glaze for his esthetic effect. Each piece was therefore unique, its surface decoration, rather than its form, determining its artistry. Pieces which were individually thrown were identified as Grand Feu Art Pottery, and those which were cast as Brauckman Art Pottery. Glazes were listed as Turquoise, Mission, Tiger's Eye, Blue, Yellow, Green and Blue Ramose, Moss Agate, and so on.[59] The vase illustrated here (69) is highly exceptional, incorporating its glazes in a series of bands which resemble a saleman's sample. Its form, too, is uncharacteristic; the lobes breaking with the classical shapes of the pottery's standard output.

The University City Pottery
Taxile Doat

Brauckman's inspiration in the use of *grès* may have been Taxile Doat (1851–1939) – one of the leading turn-of-the-century potters who used *grès* and who in 1905 published a book on the subject, *Grand Feu Ceramics.*[60] Half a generation older than most of the American Arts and Crafts potters whose work is discussed in this book, Doat was a legendary figure by the early years of this century. Famous for his mastery of the *pâte-sur-pâte* technique at the National Manufactory of Sèvres, for which he shared prominence in France with Léon Solon, Doat's work in *flambé*, crystalline, and metallic glazes was also reviewed frequently in *Keramic Studio* by Adelaide Robineau.[61] The form of a vase of 1914 (70), designed by Doat at the University City Pottery, University City, Missouri, evolves from a series based on the gourd, colocynth (bitter apple), and other themes from Nature, which Doat created around 1900. It appears that he brought his molds with him when he came to the United States, as some of the models which he produced at University City vary only in size – they are slightly smaller – from the French prototypes, a fact probably explained by the greater shrinkage of American clay. Doat's choice of glazes for these fruit- and vegetable-form vases changed at University City from the earth tones he had preferred in France to the more exotic *flambé* surface texture enriched with the crystalline decoration shown here. Parts of the porcelain body were left unglazed to show its intrinsic beauty

Doat was drawn to University City by Edward J. Lewis, a local entrepreneur and art lover, who founded the American Women's League in 1907 to educate women and broaden their professional opportunities. The League offered courses in business, languages, journalism, photography, and art, the last-mentioned including a heavy emphasis on pottery, for which Lewis had developed a great passion after reading Doat's book.

In 1909 Doat traveled to University City to advise the League's architect on "the erection of one of the most perfectly designed and equipped art potteries in the world." Later that year, having returned to Paris to gather

70   *Vase, designed by Taxile Doat at the University City Pottery (1914). Porcelain. Of ribbed and shouldered octagonal form. The shaded cream glaze is heightened with random yellow crystalline formations and traces of pale blue, the porcelain body left unglazed in places. 10¼in. (26cm.) high; 1¹³⁄₁₆in. (4.6cm.) diameter of base.*
Private Collection

his personal collection of pottery, which Lewis had purchased, Doat took up the position of head of the University City Pottery. Production began in April 1910. For a glorious moment the Pottery boasted some of the most prestigious names in the medium: Doat, Robineau, Rhead, and Dahlquist, all attracted by its ultramodern facilities. The League foundered in 1911, however, though Doat continued his work through 1914, balancing a range of low-fire commercial wares with a selection of experimental pieces. He returned in 1915 to France.

Adelaide Alsop Robineau

Adelaide Alsop Robineau (1865–1929), who is considered to be America's consummate artist/craftsman, joined the University City Pottery in 1910, by which time she had already achieved a considerable reputation as a potter.

A "Viking Ship" vase (72) of 1908 was her second version of the same subject. It can be assumed that the initial model (dated around 1905) had been destroyed.[62] The vase's theme of Nordic sailing boats has been described as representative of the artist's Art Nouveau period, but the imagery is not Art Nouveau so much as "decorative," in the late Victorian and Edwardian manner. In fact, Robineau took the design from a 1901 border design by H. E. Simpson illustrated in *Dekorative Vorbilder*.[63] In 1908, Robineau made the "Crab" vase, which was similar in shape and decoration to the Viking model, the band of crabs at the shoulder matched by a pierced band on the ring base.

Robineau created her sculptured detailing by excising, that is, by paring away, the background until the primary images stood out in relief. The same effect could have been achieved by the *pâte-sur-pâte* technique mastered by Taxile Doat, with whom Robineau was briefly associated at University City. Her preference for excising was explained in the booklet accompanying her entries to the Panama-Pacific Exposition: "She prefers excising, not only because it is more artistic, but also because it is more difficult. In her work she seems to enjoy more than anything else the struggle against difficulties." This characteristic of her work – the propensity always to choose techniques with the least probability of success, was criticized by several of her ceramic colleagues, in particular Frederick H. Rhead, who wrote in a discussion of her excised work,

A frail piece of porcelain should not be carved. The risk of smashing it before the work is finished is too great. Then when the piece is finished there is another and greater risk in the firing. Another difficulty is in the glazing of such work and this is one we have not solved yet. If you glaze a carved piece with the average glaze the details are drowned and the effect of the carving is lost.[64]

Undaunted by the impracticalities of her labors, both financial and technical, Robineau continued to work with what Rhead estimated was a 4 percent probability of success.

Her "Scarab" vase of 1910–11 (71) is a *tour de force* which incorporates many of her most painstaking techniques. First, there is its method of excised detailing.[65] Porcelain has to be perfectly dry before it can be treated. To be carved, the dry paste must be carefully pared away with fine needles and scrapers. Only a minuscule amount of powder can be removed at a time as too much pressure will break or chip the clay. The process requires infinite patience and precision, qualities which Robineau had in abundance. The carved detailing alone on the Scarab vase took four months of steady work – roughly 1,000 hours – much of it in 12-hour sessions. Often the only evidence of progress at the end of the day was "on an otherwise clean floor there would be about enough dry porcelain dust to cover a dollar piece, and half an inch more carving on the vase."[66] The same design executed on a pottery, rather than porcelain, vase, can be easily and safely modeled in a damp state within a matter of days.

The glaze on the Scarab vase represented a new departure for Robineau. Previously she had relied mainly on mat, crystalline, or flammé glazes. Here, though, apparently for the first time, she tried a semi-opaque glaze which retains its translucency, without too much brilliance, when fired at cone 9 (2400°F). The background of the vase was left unglazed so that when the piece is held to the light, it appears distinctly white and translucent. This effect was made possible by the inclusion of a thin Texas kaolin clay in the porcelain mixture with which the vase was made. Normally, for works fired at this high temperature, a stoneware, rather than porcelain, formula is used to prevent damage in the kiln. Stoneware, however, lacks the innate translucency of porcelain, an effect sought by Robineau in this piece.

The artist's husband, Samuel Robineau, described the vase's theme as "the beetle or scarab pushing a ball of food, symbolizing the toiler and his work. The interpretation of the design is as follows: the toiler, taking pride and pleasure in his work, holds it up, striving always toward the ideal, typified by the carved sphere within sphere which surmounts the cover."[67] Mr. Robineau apparently missed the symbolic significance of the ball of dung (which he referred to as "food") in which the beetle implants its egg, which, after it has been hardened by the sun, the beetle buries in the ground. When the larva hatches, it makes its way to the earth's surface to renew the beetle's life cycle.

The extreme fragility of Robineau's technique is shown in the fact that the Scarab vase was almost destroyed in its last stage of creation. It emerged from its second, and final, firing with a series of deep cracks around the base, some of which were so serious that Taxile Doat, who was present at the kiln, felt that it could not be salvaged.[68] But Robineau arduously filled the cracks with a composition of powdered porcelain and flux, and then reglazed and refired it. When it emerged again from the kiln the flaws were undetectable. Other masterpieces were less fortunate. The larger Sea Garden vase, for example, elaborately carved with turtles and seaweed for display at the 1915 Panama-Pacific Exposition in San Francisco, had to be discarded twice; the first time when it broke at the completion of the carving process, and the second when it was spoiled by an accident in its second firing. By the time Robineau began her third attempt, she had already spent about six months of uninterrupted, and fruitless, time on the piece.[69]

The "Fox and Grapes" covered jar (73, 74) was created in the last decade of Robineau's life, at the moment when the post-World War I Parisian Modernist style was introduced into the United States. Robineau was

Left

71 "Scarab" Vase ('The Apotheosis of the
Toiler'), designed and executed by Adelaide
Alsop Robineau, University City Pottery
(1910/11).
Excised, perforated, and glazed porcelain.
The baluster body has a matching cover and
pedestal foot. Decorated with rows of carved
scarab beetles intersected by perforated scarab
medallions. The ground is in semiopaque
white glaze with traces of green, the
medallions in a darker turquoise green glaze.
16⅝in. (42.2cm.) high.
Collection of the Everson Museum of Art,
Syracuse, New York. Photo Courtney Frisse

Opposite right

72 "Viking ship" Vase, designed and executed by Adelaide Alsop Robineau, Syracuse (1908).
Excised, perforated, and glazed porcelain. The baluster body is decorated at the shoulder with a band of Viking ships sailing to the right. In rich mat and semi-mat blue, green, brown, and cream glazes. The pierced ring base is similarly decorated. 7¼in. (18.4cm.) high.
Collection of the Everson Museum of Art, Syracuse, New York. Photo Courtney Frisse

Below and right

73, 74 "Fox and Grapes" Jar, with cover, designed and executed by Adelaide Alsop Robineau, Syracuse (1922).
Excised and glazed porcelain. The obverse and reverse have upper and lower excised medallions depicting foxes feeding from pendant grape-laden vines within incised concentric lines in a bronze black mat glaze. The 2 flanking shield-shaped cartouches are glazed in mottled beige with concentric broken pale blue bands. 7¼in. (8.4cm.) high; 5in. (12.7cm.) diameter.
Private Collection, Courtesy of The Jordan-Volpe Gallery, New York

reluctant to embrace the new style and her work remained essentially conservative until the end.[70] It is interesting, therefore, to note the small compromise to Modernism in this jar: its form and glazing technique are traditional, but the foxes are rendered in a lightly angular manner which reveals the artist's awareness of the up-to-the-minute stylizations at the Paris Salons, an awareness she acquired through the foreign decorative arts reviews, especially *Art et Décoration*. Robineau's early designs, shown in the graphic sketches she included in her publication *Keramic Studio* from 1899 onwards, were Art Nouveau inspired, drawing on the floral vernacular of designers such as Paul Follot, Maurice Dufrène, and Eugène Grasset. By 1910, however, the vibrant *fin de siècle* French influence had faded from her work, yielding frequently to Chinese, American Indian, and Mayan motifs.

Typical of her profession, Robineau kept the formulae of her glazes for high-fire porcelains a close secret during her lifetime. Endless research and experimentation – empirical rather than scientific – led to a wide range of mat, glossy, and crystalline glazed effects. These were applied with a brush made of a very soft animal hair, which gave her some control and flexibility (she preferred the brush technique to the alternate means of glaze application: immersion, spraying, and sponging). The application of the glaze to the shield-shaped panels on this vase is typical of the manner in which the artist "floated" it on to the piece without letting the bristles touch the surface. Three applications ensured an even coating of glaze that stood out fully from the body of the vase.

On Robineau's death on 18 February 1929, her obituary in the *New York Herald Tribune* noted that she combined "taste and technique magnificently fused." Her success can be gauged by the numerous prizes and citations she was awarded, both in Europe and the United States, the former an international forum in which no other individual American ceramicist was considered worthy of participation. In a rare tribute, the Metropolitan Museum of Art mounted a retrospective exhibition of her porcelains in the year of her death; three years later, Anna Wetherill Olmsted, director of the Syracuse Museum of Fine Arts, inaugurated a series of Ceramic National Exhibitions in her memory.

Frederick Hurten Rhead

Frederick Hurten Rhead (1880–1942) was also associated with the University City Pottery. It was there in 1911 that he designed and executed the vase illustrated here (75). Its imagery is extremely appealing, both in its theme and selection of sharply contrasting colors. Its style recalls the flat, two-dimensional technique applied by turn-of-the-century poster artists such as Eugène Grasset in France and William Bradley in the United States. The panorama of blossom-laden trees and mushrooms corresponds to the prevailing Art Nouveau philosophy, its interpretation on this vase recalling similar models in glass, both of forests and mushrooms, by the movement's premier *verrier*, Emile Gallé.

The vase provides an example of Rhead's best known technique, which he had introduced at Roseville in Zanesville, Ohio, when he was the pottery's art

Right

75 Vase, designed and executed by
Frederick Hurten Rhead at the University
City Pottery (1911).
Ceramics. Of elongated baluster shape with
flaring rim, decorated with a forest scene of
mushrooms beneath tall trees, in white, green,
blue, and brown glazes with incised outline
detailing. 17½in. (44.4cm.) high; 4¾in.
(12.7cm.) diameter.
Collection of P. G. Pugsley & Sons Antiques,
San Francisco, California. Photo Robert
Reiter

Below

76 Low Bowl, designed and executed by
Frederick Hurten Rhead at the Rhead Pottery
(c.1915).
Ceramics. A circular bowl, decorated with a
central scarab beetle clutching spheres in
mottled brown and pink on a mirror-black
ground, within a border of stylized lotus
sprays. 8¾in. (22.2cm.) diameter.
Collection of The Oakland Museum,
Oakland, California. Gift of the Estate of
Helen Hathaway White. Photo Joe Samberg

director between 1904 and 1908, and which he continued to employ after moving to California in 1913. Paul Evans has described the process,

This was effected by painting the decoration in outline, then applying the background slip and finally filling in the decoration with slips of various different colors – all while the piece was not harder than green. The ware was allowed to dry to a hard green condition; then, using a sharp-toothed tool, the slip was cut back either to the outline color or to the body itself.[71]

Rhead was born in Staffordshire, England, where he succeeded his father as director of the Wardle Art Pottery in Hanley, before coming to the United States in 1902.[72] After working at various potteries, he became pottery instructor at the University City Pottery in 1909, where he was associated with Taxile Doat and Adelaide Robineau. In 1911 he joined the Arequipa Pottery, two years later setting off for Southern California to establish the Camarata Pottery in Santa Barbara's Mission Canyon. This was later incorporated as the Rhead Pottery.

Rhead retained an Italian thrower to produce the large pots (between 12 and 20 in number and averaging three feet in height) that he created daily for garden ornaments. He also hired an English thrower to create a range of smaller pieces, which allowed him to concentrate on design and decoration. In this, he was assisted by his wife, Agnes Rhead, Lois Whitcomb (later his second wife), and some of his students.

A low bowl of around 1915 (76) incorporates Rhead's most distinct creation, his mirror-black glaze, which he perfected after fifteen years of research into the techniques of ancient Chinese mirrored glazes. He claimed to have experimented with more than 11,000 different formulae before being fully satisfied.

The plate's scarab and lotus motifs show another of Rhead's influences, that of Egyptology, which has been introduced here into a design which identifies itself also with Robineau's "Scarab" vase, which Rhead had seen at the University City Pottery four or five years earlier.

Rhead was particularly fond of the form of this bowl, which he decorated with themes such as flowers, peacocks, and abstract imagery. The decoration, applied often in repeating patterns such as in the lotus leaves on this bowl, was invariably incised.

In contrast to his great skills as an artist and technician, Rhead proved a poor businessman. His two prime projects – the Rhead Pottery and *The Potter*, the latter a monthly magazine which he launched to cover all aspects of the pottery industry – were both abandoned in 1917. Soon after this, he became director of research at the American Encaustic Tiling Company in Zanesville, a position he retained until 1927, when he resigned to join the Homer Laughlin China Company in West Virginia, for which he designed the firm's "Fiesta" dinnerware.

George E. Ohr

George E. Ohr (1857–1918) was born in Biloxi, Mississippi, and became known as "The Mad Biloxi Potter." In the summer of 1875, he traveled to New Orleans to apprentice under Joseph Meyer, who later became master potter at Newcomb Pottery. Ohr set up his own studio in Biloxi in 1893.

Right

77   Vase, designed and executed by George
E. Ohr (1900–06).
Ceramics. Of baluster shape, with a central
band of crimped indentations beneath a
bulbous shoulder. The metallic black high
glaze is heightened with charcoal speckling.
13⅝in. (33.7cm.) high; 5⁵⁄₁₆in. (13.5cm.)
diameter of base.
Private Collection

Below

78   Vase, designed and executed by George
E. Ohr (1900–06).
Ceramics. Of baluster shape, with 4 deeply
frilled bands beneath a ruffled rim. The
brown glaze is speckled to black on the frills.
8¼in. (21cm.) high; 3⁵⁄₁₆in. (8.4cm.)
diameter of base
Private Collection

His technical virtuosity grew rapidly as he personally threw, glazed, and fixed all his works. His search for new shapes led to his much-vaunted claim of "No two alike."

Ohr used local clays, particularly from the nearby Tchootibuffe River, fired at a low temperature. "The decoration of an Ohr pot grows out of the clay," noted Robert W. Blasberg in his book on Ohr. "It *is* the clay. There is no reliance on pictorialism. There are no medallions like Mettlach, no organic natural form like Van Briggle, beautiful though these devices undoubtedly are."[73]

Ohr concentrated on form and glaze. With regard to his dexterity with the former, Paul E. Cox wrote, "It is said Ohr could work on the wheel whichever way it turned. Certainly he could throw wares of considerable size with walls much thinner than any potter ever has accomplished. It is quite probable that George Ohr, rated simply as a mechanic, was the most expert thrower the craft has ever known."[74] Pieces were thrown and manipulated into crushed, twisted, folded, dented, and pinched shapes with ease and abandon. Forms were fanciful, sometimes almost acrobatic.

To these frequently bizarre forms, Ohr applied a kaleidoscope of glazes. Early splotched, speckled, and mottled effects were joined later by dark glazes, especially metallic and crystalline varieties, which were often combined on a single piece.

His baluster-shaped vase of 1900–06 (77) appears to have been thrown in two parts – the upper neck and shoulder section, and the lower half – as Ohr could not have inserted his hand inside the narrow mouth to help shape the lower portion as he shaped it on the wheel. The logical joint appears at the waist, above the band of indentations. The resulting form is interesting and comprises, in effect, one vase superimposed on another. Its basic form evolves from the baluster vase of antiquity, to which Ohr has applied a favorite glaze, his mirrored black variety, in a slightly uneven manner that allows the clay body to show through in places. A ruffled type of decoration appears in a vase (78) of around the same period. The pleats were applied to a simple body shape and then glazed and fired, giving the impression that the vase was "crushed."

Three baluster-shaped vases from the 1900–10 period show the range of Ohr's glaze techniques (79), in two instances applied in different colors to the front and back of the piece. They illustrate also wheel-turned shapes that lack Ohr's more extreme manipulations. The narrow neck and flaring rim of a vase created in the early 1900s (80) appear as a second pot superimposed on top of the bulbous body. The exaggerated pair of wing handles (fashioned by hand) add flamboyance to the brightly colored glaze, which was sponge-applied to achieve a variegated effect.

A teapot of 1900–06 (81) combines Ohr's two most distinctive characteristics: an irregular shape and an experimental glaze, the latter in this instance with a rare spattered red finish. Ohr threw the body of the teapot by hand but used a mold for the spout.[75] It is uncertain whether Ohr's teapots were designed to be used, since the low-fire earthenware, of which this model is made, is fragile and liable to develop fissures in its firing. More likely they belong to his whimsical work, the range of puzzle mugs and novelty items classified today as "gimcracks."

79 (Left) Vase, designed and executed by George E. Ohr (1900).
Ceramics. Baluster-shaped with twin handles, the rim with 9 diagonal crimped lobes above a band of pinched and twisted indentations on the shoulder and a twisted band at the waist. The obverse in an uneven dark blue high glaze decorated with silvery black speckling and splashed accents; the reverse in a deep aubergine/purple high glaze heightened with silver-centered green dots. 11½in. (29.2cm.) high; 4⁵⁄₁₆in. (10.9cm.) diameter of foot.
Collection of R. A. Ellison

(Center) Vase, designed and executed by George E. Ohr (1900–06).
Ceramics. Baluster-shaped, applied with twin openwork handles. The obverse is in a streaked and mottled aubergine and purple high glaze decorated with speckled dark green vertical bands heightened with silver-gray dots and spatterings; the reverse has an identical glaze on the upper half and a mottled dark aubergine and plum glaze on the lower half; the interior is in a brownish beige glaze with green spotting. 10⅜in. (26.4cm.) high; 3½in. (8.9cm.) diameter of base.
Collection of Mr. and Mrs. Jack B. Hartog

(Right) Vase, designed and executed by George E. Ohr (1900–10).
Ceramics. Baluster shaped, applied with elaborately scrolled double handles. The gray-green glaze is heightened with a profusion of green speckles, random gunmetal gray dots, and reddish burgundy mottling. The interior has 3 drips of green glaze extending downwards over a brown glaze. 9¹¹⁄₁₆in. (24.6cm.) high; 3⅜in. (8.6cm.) diameter of base.
Collection of R. A. Ellison

80 *Vase, designed and executed by George E. Ohr (1900–06).*
Ceramics. A baluster-shaped vase, with applied reticulated "wing" handles and twisted foot decoration; applied with a mottled maroon, green, and blue high glaze, several parts of the clay body exposed through the glaze. 12½in. (31.8cm.) high; 4⅞in. (12.4cm.) diameter of base.
Private Collection

81 *Teapot, designed and executed by George E. Ohr (1900–06).*
Ceramics. The body has pinched indentations, and an applied snake-form spout and whiplash handle. The deep claret glaze is applied with random pinkish-beige splotches, several with burst surfaces revealing a gray cellular interior. The knopped circular lid is similarly decorated on the exterior and has a greenish brown interior. 7in. (17.8cm.) high; 3⁵⁄₁₆in. (8.4cm.) diameter of foot.
Jederman Collection, N.A.

Most contemporary commentary placed Ohr's work somewhere between folk and high art. While Grueby was praised for simplifying his forms, Ohr was criticized for distorting his, and for over-ornamentation. His glazes, though, were universally acclaimed. As the critic Edwin Atlee Barber wrote in 1904, "The principal quality of the ware consists in the richness of the glazes, which are wonderfully varied, the reds, greens, and metallic luster effects being particularly good."[76]

In keeping with his nonconformism, Ohr renounced glazes in his later years, claiming that his ceramic genius was independent of color or "quality." In 1906, he closed his pottery operation and his remaining inventory, between six and eight thousand pieces, remained in the family warehouse, forgotten by the pottery world, until the early 1970s.[77]

The Marblehead Pottery

The Marblehead Pottery was formed in 1904 by Dr. Herbert J. Hall, as part of his therapeutic community.[78] His weaving, basketry and pottery classes established him as a pioneer in what is now termed occupational therapy. In 1905 Arthur Eugene Baggs was retained to oversee the pottery program. It soon expanded into a profitable commercial undertaking, producing a distinct range of ceramic wares. In 1915 Baggs purchased the pottery, now fully established with outlets throughout the country and numerous awards to its name.

The style of most pieces from Marblehead was characterized by austere classical forms, muted colors, mat glazes, and restrained decoration. Baggs has forsaken this style in his vase of 1925 (82) for an artistic and technical *tour de force* in which the detailing is provided by sgraffito. The vase's decoration is surprising in its adherence to an Art Nouveau floral esthetic which reached its peak of popularity a quarter century earlier. It is especially surprising as in the same year Baggs joined the Cowan Pottery, run by Guy Cowan, who almost singlehandedly promoted the Parisian high-style form of Modernism known today as "Art Deco."

By the time the Marblehead Pottery closed, in 1936, it is estimated to have produced at least 200,000 pieces of ceramics.

The Overbeck Pottery

The Overbeck Pottery was a family concern run by the Overbeck sisters: Margaret, Hannah, Elizabeth, and Mary.[79] A vase of 1930–35 (83) was a collaboration between Elizabeth and Mary. Elizabeth, the second eldest daughter, studied under Charles F. Binns at the College for Clayworking and Ceramics in Alfred, New York, in 1909–10. She was technically the most gifted of the four, channeling her efforts into pottery by working at the wheel and experimenting with clays and glazes. Mary, the youngest, studied initially under the eldest, Margaret, and later under Arthur Dow and Marshall Fry at Columbia University. She had a long and varied career as a designer, artist, and potter. Examples of her floral designs were illustrated repeatedly in 1904–16 issues of *Keramic Studio*. Birds, the theme of this vase, became her dominant interest after 1916.

82   *Vase, designed by Arthur Eugene Baggs,*
the Marblehead Pottery (1925).
An urn-shaped vase, decorated with a
sgraffito design of wisteria vines in turquoise
blue over teal blue on a high gloss blue-black
ground. 5¼in. (14cm.) high; 5⅜in. (13.2cm.)
diameter.
Collection of the Newark Museum, Newark,
New Jersey

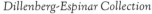

83 *Vase, designed by Mary Frances Overbeck and modeled by Elizabeth Overbeck, the Overbeck Pottery (1930–35). Incised and glazed ceramics. The baluster-shaped body is decorated with 2 rows of 5 blue birds among stylized flower clusters in cranberry, yellow, and blue on a chequered green and caramel ground; all with incised detailing. 8in. (20.3cm.) high; 4in. (10.2cm.) diameter of foot; 4⅞in. (12.4cm.) diameter of top.*
Dillenberg-Espinar Collection

The vase was probably made between the years 1930 and 1935. Its geometric stylization and muted palette are pure Paris a decade earlier, similar to decorated ceramics produced by Primavera, Pomone, and La Maîtrise in the early 1920s, known today broadly as "high Art Deco."

Each Overbeck piece underwent an elaborate handcrafted procedure. As Kathleen R. Postle explained in her comprehensive book on the family,

Each piece has a design, first worked out on paper, usually done in glaze inlay either alone or combined with incising or carving when the clay is in leatherhard condition. The design was traced on, then outlined, etched in lines carved in the surface, or incised, so that cutting away part of the surface created a bas-relief. This was done by one of several handmade tools, with pewter or copper tip, shaped to a narrow chisel end. In the second method, when the piece was dried to leather hardness, the incising was so done that the design was outlined and made to stand out from the surface, or carved out, in the manner of intaglio. Some pieces show the sgraffito process, incising through the top slip to reveal a pattern on contrasting background (to be distinguished from simple incising in the body of the ware).[80]

In an attempt to depart from the realism of traditional china painting, which they associated with nineteenth-century ceramic decoration, the Overbecks used the incised line to divide the vessel's surface into blocks of separate color, "Emphasis was on line enclosing shape, shape emphasizing line, without regard to naturalistic conventions of depth-perspective."[81] The abstract stylizations of 1920s Paris gave the Overbecks an effective and fashionable means of applying their philosophy when the French style finally arrived in the Midwest towards the end of the decade.

3   *Metal and Silver*

Initially the American metalworker of the Arts and Crafts Movement drew his inspiration directly from his medieval counterpart. The craft remained firmly bound to fundamentals: only the hammer and essential chasing tools were considered legitimate, their stroke marks left proudly on the metal's surface as proof of its maker's manual dexterity. Structural elements, such as chamfered rivets, were frequently left exposed to provide a small decorative fillip.

The Arts and Crafts silver industry, both the single artisan and larger firms, embraced the same philosophy, though greater public demand for silverware led to the widespread use of machinery, such as stamping presses, to expedite production. The relative simplicity required in working with silver or metal, and the small amount of space necessary to do so, spawned a wide "cottage" industry. Artisans such as Jarvie and Van Erp initially worked part-time at home. The work of many other hobbyists, of a comparable technical standard but unsigned, appears on today's market.

Gustav Stickley

As the movement progressed, however, metalwork designers became more and more conscious of influences from abroad. Gustav Stickley, whose importance in the field of furniture has already been noted, prided himself, both in print and in many speeches, on the strength of the bond forged between himself and William Morris's disciples. The earlier furniture, in particular, bears close structural resemblances to models developed by Arthur Mackmurdo, C.F.A. Voysey, and M.H. Baillie Scott.

In 1905, Stickley established a metalwork department to supplement his cabinet shop. The stamped hardware that he had first used did not suit the solid, handcrafted appearance of the furniture, so a blacksmithy was set up to forge handwrought hinges, key escutcheons, and handles. Lamp fixtures, fireplace furniture, chafing dishes, coal buckets, and other objects were soon in production, as well as accessories in copper, brass, and wrought-iron.

Architectural elements, such as fireplace hoods and balustrades, allowed Stickley to achieve his ambition – a fully integrated Arts and Crafts interior.

Early in 1903, Stickley hosted an exhibition of metalwork by the Art Fittings Company of Birmingham, England, in the Craftsman Building, Syracuse. Several *repoussé* copper chargers, mirror frames, and wall plaques were included, and a number of these copper pieces were influenced by the English Arts and Crafts Movement. The copper wall plaque (84) was illustrated in Stickley's *Craftsman Story* (1905). It has a recessed center decorated with *repoussé* spade-like forms on the broad border, and a hand-hammered textured finish. Stickley himself attributed this design to the influence of Harvey Ellis.

84 (Center) Wall Plaque, model no. 344, designed by Gustav Stickley, executed at the Craftsman Workshops (1905–10). Hand-wrought copper. The recessed center is decorated with 4 "repoussé" spade-like motifs. The entire surface has a hand-hammered textured finish. 15⅛in. (38.4cm.) diameter. Private Collection

(Left) Inkwell, designed and executed by Dirk Van Erp (1912–15). Hand-wrought copper with glass liner. The overhanging square and domed lid is decorated with a twin band of broken lines along the rim. The protruding front edge opens to a square detachable interior enclosing a glass liner. 3¼in. (8.2cm.) high; 4⁵⁄₁₆in. (11cm.) diameter of lid excluding protruding edge. Collection of Mr. and Mrs. John M. Angelo

(Right) Bud vase, designed by Karl Kipp at the Roycroft Copper Shop (c.1911). Copper and German silver. The cylindrical body is supported by 4 buttressed arms and decorated at the rim with 4 applied squares in German silver. 8in. (20.3cm.) high; 4¼in. (10.8cm.) diameter at the foot, including arms; 1¹¹⁄₁₆in. (4.3cm.) diameter of mouth. Collection of Gabriela Brown, New York

85 *Jardinière, model no. 278, designed by Gustav Stickley, executed at the Craftsman Workshops (c.1905).*
Hand-wrought copper and wrought-iron. Cylindrical, with flaring rim. The jardinière is supported by 2 wrought-iron hoops raised on 4 scrolled feet and applied with twin handles. 14in. (35.5cm.) high; 11¹³⁄₁₆in. (30cm.) diameter of top rim; 14¾in. (37.5cm.) diameter of foot.
Collection of Gabriela Brown, New York

A jardinière produced around the same time to Stickley's design (85) is closer in inspiration to some of his early furniture. It exemplifies the robust, handcrafted effect aspired to by Arts and Crafts exponents.

Dirk Van Erp

Dirk Van Erp (1860–1933) was born in Leewarden, Holland, and after an apprenticeship with his father – a commercial coppersmith – he emigrated to the U.S.A., gaining employment as a coppersmith in the naval shipyards on Mare Island near San Francisco. His metalwork began as a hobby, and he never shook off a somewhat rudimentary, self-taught style, but he had a fine sensitivity to form and proportion.

His Copper Shop, which he established in Oakland in 1908 and which he moved in 1910 to San Francisco, was flourishing by 1915.

An inkwell of handwrought copper (84) and a vase (86) date from the prewar period (1910–15). The vase is Japanesque in its serenity, simplicity, and honesty to materials. Its relatively large size required Van Erp to employ a vertical seam, which he gave a mat, dentilled finish. The brown patina of the vase is highlighted with areas of reddish-brown, which Van Erp achieved by the application of a rutile solution (titanium dioxide).

In the second half of World War I, Van Erp again took up naval shipyard work, leaving his children to oversee his designs. After the war, he returned, and remained until his retirement in 1929. It was during this period that he designed the copper vase (87) whose vigorous *martelé* decorative finish shows the metalworker's craft at its most complex and arduous. The finish was achieved by the application of alternative hammer strokes to its inside and outside surfaces. Elizabeth Eleanor D'Arcy Gaw (1868–1944), briefly Van Erp's partner in the years 1910–11, collaborated with him on this vase.[1]

Van Erp participated in several exhibitions during his career, including the Alaska-Yukon-Pacific Exposition in Seattle (1909), and the Panama-Pacific International Exposition in San Francisco (1915).

Roycroft

Jerome Stanley Connor joined Roycroft in 1898, within a year producing a single edition of terracotta busts and plaques. It was he who sculpted the pair of andirons (88), which were illustrated in *The Philistine* in 1899, accompanied by the legend: "St. Jerome – Roycroft made "em: This pair of Andirons all out of good black iron! – the loving marks of the hammer still upon them ... Price, well say $18.00."[2]

The andirons were designed by William Wallace Denslow as seahorses, for use in the Roycroft buildings; both the Ruskin Room in the Inn and the Chapel have contained sets at different times. The model, produced also in a modified version sculpted by Peter Robarge, became one of the earliest craft items offered by the Roycroft blacksmith shop to the general public. Roughly ten pairs are believed to exist today.

Denslow was employed by Hubbard, Roycroft's founder, in 1897, to teach local girls the art of book illuminating.[3] In addition to the design of the

Below left

86 Vase, designed and executed by Dirk Van Erp (1910–15).
Copper. Of gently tapering cyclindrical form with incurved rim, the large, hand-hammered body joined with a single dentilled seam. 23⅝in. (60cm.) high; 10in. (25.4cm.) diameter.
Collection of Susan Fetterolf and Jeffrey Gorin

Below right

87 Vase, designed and executed by Dirk Van Erp (1915–20).
Copper. Of flattened spherical form with collared rim and applied foot; decorated with a pronounced wart-like knopped finish and chocolate brown patination. 10⅜in. (26.3cm.) high; 9¼in. (23.5cm.) diameter.
Collection of Gabriela Brown, New York

seahorse watermark applied to the imported English and European hand-made paper used by Roycroft in its earliest books, Denslow oversaw the ornamentation and design of the volumes themselves. He incorporated the same seahorse, which he called a Hippocampus, into his signature for book illustrations and cartoons for *The Philistine* and *The Fra*.[4] Denslow left Roycroft in 1907, later achieving celebrity as the illustrator of *The Wizard of Oz*.

Karl Kipp, who joined Roycroft in 1908, was responsible for transforming the existing metal-making facility into a cohesive, and profitable, operation. The shop eventually included thirty-five artisans with a range of more than 150 items. Kipp, a former banker and self-taught craftsman, designed the items, turning his sketches over to assistants for their execution.

The pierced square design on the copper band of his jardinière (89) takes its inspiration directly from the *Quadrant* motif in the decorative wares of Josef Hoffmann, Otto Czeschka, and Koloman Moser at the Wiener Werkstätte in the early years of this century. These, in turn, had been derived from the checkerboard designs incorporated by Charles Rennie Mackintosh in his Glasgow chair and wallpaper designs. Kipp was introduced to the works of the Europeans by Dard Hunter who, even before his visit to Vienna in 1908, was greatly influenced by the Austrian Secession movement.

A bud vase of around 1911 (84) is uncharacteristic of Kipp's work. It incorporates a thick section of copper piping which has been heavily planished by hand to create a vertical pattern. The four silvered squares contrast strongly with the rich copper tones of the vase's red-brown patina. The model was first illustrated in *The Fra*, November 1911, priced at $5.

Kipp is not believed to have applied his own signature, an encircled *KK*, to the metalware that he designed for Roycroft. Only the pieces that he created in the four years of existence of his own studio, the Tookay Shop (established in 1912) bear his signature. Certain Kipp pieces do, however, incorporate both his and the Roycroft mark – these are pieces of unsold stock from the Tookay Shop which he took back to Roycroft when he returned to his former position in 1915, and where the Roycroft logo was added before the pieces were put back on the market.[5]

Contemporary Roycroft literature does not identify the designer of a handhammered cigarette box created in the early 1920s (90). Though it is not characteristic of Kipp's style, nor the style of Walter H. Jennings, another Roycroft designer, it incorporates a quality of design and exemplary artisanship indicative of their work.[6]

In a 1925 Roycroft catalogue, *The Book of the Roycrofters*, a set of matching pieces, including a covered cigar and cigarette tray, are illustrated with the caption: "In the Verde green Finish, reminiscent of age-old bronzes sought after and beloved by antiquarians." The traces of green in this box – particularly on the interior, which has retained much of its original finish – indicate that the original green patination has gradually been removed through use and cleaning.

By early 1912 Kipp had left Roycroft to set up The Tookay Shop, in East Aurora. After Hubbard's death in 1915, Bert Hubbard enticed him back to his former position as Head of the Copper Shop.

Opposite above

88 *Pair of Andirons, designed by William Wallace Denslow, executed by Jerome Stanley Connor, at the Roycroft Shops (1902–04).*
Designed as seahorses, the front feet linked by a horizontal bar to the single rear foot. 22¼in. (56.5cm.) high; 22in. (55.9cm.) length to rear foot; 8in. (20.3cm.) width of front feet.
Private Collection

Opposite, below left

89 *Jardinière/Fern Dish, designed by Karl Kipp at the Roycroft Copper Shop (1910–11).*
Hammered copper and brass. The cylindrical copper body is applied at the neck with a brass band pierced with twin rows of squares. The 4 square feet are surmounted with ball finials and applied with circular bail handles. 8⁵⁄₁₆in. (21.1cm.) diameter of jardinière, excluding feet; 7⅞in. (20cm.) high; 9¼in. (23.5cm.) diameter, including feet.
Collection of The Metropolitan Museum of Art. Purchase, Theodore R. Gamble, Jr. Gift, in honor of his mother, Mrs. Theodore Robert Gamble, 1982

Opposite, below right

90 *Cigarette Box, the Roycroft Copper Shop (probably early 1920s).*
Hand-hammered copper, the brown patina with traces of verdigris on the rear and on the interior. The lid is applied with 2 hinges designed as conventionalized leaf sprays. 1¼in. (3.2cm.) high; 6¹¹⁄₁₆in. (17cm.) long; 3½in. (8.9cm.) deep.
Collection of Tod M. Volpe

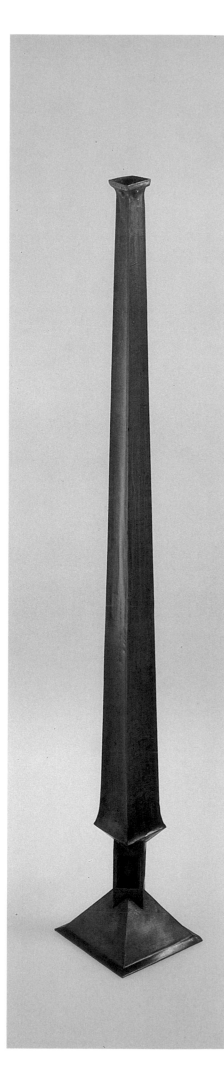

Left

91 "Weed-holder" Vase, designed by Frank Lloyd Wright, executed by James A. Miller, Chicago (1893–1902).
Copper, hand-wrought. An elongated tapering square vessel with a flaring rim, raised on a square support with recessed panels decorated in their centers with oval obtrusions. 29½in. (74.9cm.) high; 4¼in. (10.8cm.) diameter of foot
Collection of the Carnegie Museum of Art, Pittsburgh, Pennsylvania. DuPuy Fund

Below

92 Urn, designed by Frank Lloyd Wright for the Dana house, Springfield, Illinois, executed by James A. Miller (c.1903).
Copper and galvanized tin. A spherical urn on a 4-part foot; decorated with 4 "repoussé" circular motifs with thumb-print detailing within geometric borders. 18in. (45.7cm.) high; 18in. (45.7cm.) diameter.
Private Collection. Photo courtesy Christie's, New York

Frank Lloyd Wright

It was probably only shortly after Wright established his own practice (in 1893) that he designed a "weed-holder" vase, executed by James A. Miller (91). According to his son, John Lloyd Wright, the architect "was not satisfied with the bric-a-brac of the day, so he designed his own . . . the weed-holders . . . are his early creations. Father liked weeds!"[7] Wright subsequently included the model in several of his interiors, including the octagonal library in his own studio in Oak Park and, later, the dining room of the Dana house in Springfield.[8]

The Dana house also included among its furnishings a copper and galvanized tin urn, again executed by James A. Miller (92). The urn was one of Wright's favorite objects, appearing – with minor decorative variations – in several of his interiors. It is known that at least six were made: one for the Dana house, another for the Edward C. Waller house, and pairs for both Wright's own studio and the Coonley house. These were part of a large group of vases, urns, candlesticks, and sconces in *repoussé* copper which Wright incorporated into his Prairie School houses.[9] This example was sold at the public auction of the Dana house and its furnishings in Springfield, Illinois, in July 1943. The repeating angular geometric decoration on the vase recalls Celtic ornamentation. It also evokes certain imagery developed by Louis Sullivan for his architectural friezes.

Miller was born in St. Charles, Illinois, in 1850 and started his working life as a roofer. In 1874 he went into partnership with Abraham and Richard Knisely, working as a tinner. The firm advertised itself as specializing in "Slate, Tin & Corrugated Iron/Roofers/Manufacturers of Hayes' Patent Skylights/Elevator Buckets." Later they added slate roofs, wire glass windows, and metal frames. The firm was renamed James A. Miller & Brother in 1896. Their diverse stock and manufacturing expertise drew Wright's attention. "James A. Miller," he said, on one of the few occasions when he discussed a craftsman, "a sheet-metal worker of Chicago, had intelligent pride in his material and a sentiment concerning it. At that time I designed some sheet copper bowls, slender flower holders and such things for him, and fell in love with sheet copper as a building material . . ."

Louis Sullivan

Louis Sullivan's elevator grille of 1893–94 for the Chicago Stock Exchange (93) was part of a range of ornamental grillwork designed by Sullivan for the building's interior, which included stair railings, elevator cages, and electroliers.

In 1964, remodeling to the entrance and lobby led to the removal of the iron grilles surrounding the elevator shafts. Several of these, of which the one illustrated here is an example, have been preserved.

Sullivan's distinctive form of architectural ornamentation reached its apex in the Stock Exchange building. Apprenticed as a draftsman in the Philadelphia firm of Furness & Hewitt, Sullivan evolved his early Victorian Gothic Revival style after he joined Dankmar Adler around 1881. Adler's role in the partnership was that of engineer; Sullivan's that of building

designer. The inspiration for the decoration on the T-shaped plaque in the center of this grille can be traced to the treatise which Sullivan wrote just prior to his death in 1924, *A System of Architectural Ornament*.[10] In this he explained his method of reducing organic ornamentation to its common denominator, a "seed germ."[11] This, which he referred to as the "seat of power," took its form in the abstract oval shapes which recur in the T-shaped plaque. Sullivan described the seed germ as an embryo force. He seemed to compare the metamorphosis of a seed germ into a plant to the evolution of basic forms into creative design. The resulting combination of interlacing geometric elements and luxuriant foliage on the plaque shows Sullivan's grammar of ornamentation at its most exuberant.

The elevator grille to which the plaque is applied is less characteristic of Sullivan's decorative style. It is difficult, in fact, to find a precedent in his work for the grille's restrained symmetry of circular motifs. This suggests the influence of Frank Lloyd Wright, who had joined Adler & Sullivan in 1890 initially to ink drawings of Sullivan's designs for the Auditorium Building. By 1893, the young Wright's preference for simplified form is evident in the firm's designs for the Schiller Theater (1892–93) and the Meyer Building (1893).[12]

Tiffany & Company

Tiffany & Company showed a silver bowl with copper and niello inlay (94) at the 1893 Columbian Exposition in Chicago.[13] The bowl was part of a service, including another bowl and a pitcher, exhibited by the company. Its shape resembles a Pueblo Indian basket, and it is decorated with a more general, abstract Indian pattern.

Neither Tiffany's, nor its American competitors, used American Indian motifs with any frequency, though a similar bowl, designed after a Zuni basket, in silver with copper and turquoise inlay, was shown at the 1900 Exposition Universelle in Paris and again emphasized how suited Indian tribal motifs were to the decorative arts of the time.

Tiffany Studios

Louis Comfort Tiffany had the facility to absorb, and add to, the methods of decoration traditional to an art form. This is exemplified by his use in combination of traditional and new enameling techniques.

Tiffany appears to have set up an enamel department in 1898 as an adjunct to the studio's newly established metal furnaces.[14] On 16 February 1900, after the selection of enamelware for the new century's Exposition Universelle was shown at Tiffany Studios prior to shipment, a critic for *The Commercial Advertiser* noted "some remarkable achievements in enamel on copper, in line with the other experiments made by Mr. Tiffany, wherein he has secured all the detail, sumptuous coloring and textures of the best of the European workers, retaining a personality quite his own. This enamel is on lamps, plaques, and small boxes, and is most effective."

94 Bowl, by Tiffany & Company (1893).
Silver with copper and niello inlay. The
shoulder has 4 reserves, each chased in
"repoussé" with a desert flower above an
etched inscription: SAGE BRUSH,
GREASE WOOD, MESQUITE, and
SACRED THORN. The background is
decorated with an abstract Indian geometric
pattern in inlaid copper and niello, the
underside etched with another abstract
pattern. With gilt interior. 6¼in. (15.9cm.)
high; 12¼in. (31.1cm.) diameter.
Collection of Tiffany & Company, New
York. Photo courtesy Christie's, New York

95   Vase, Tiffany Studios (1902–05).
Enamel on copper. The copper body is
decorated with a "repoussé" design of
pendant orange branches with green foliage
on a shaded mauve and purple ground. 5⅛in.
(13cm.) high; 4⅛in. (10.5cm.) diameter of
mouth; 6½in. (16.5cm.) diameter of foot.
Collection of Los Angeles County Museum of
Art. Gift of Mr. E. H. Rose

In *The China Decorator* of April 1900, the response was similarly enthusiastic,

An entirely new and recent discovery is that of the enameling on copper, the enamel being iridescent.... This most difficult discovery seems to use the most wonderful of all, as there is nothing quite so difficult as enameling on metal in iridescent tones, an accomplishment not as yet known here, nor indeed has precisely the same method been recorded, even in the ancient history of glass.

A vase of enamel on copper of 1902–05 (95) captures an extraordinary range of colors, both in intensity and in subtle, naturalistic tones. In it, one of Tiffany's innovations is readily apparent: the application of particles of gold foil to the *repoussé* body prior to enameling. The critic Samuel Howe traced the procedure in *The Craftsman* of April 1902,

The desired relief being secured, he adds "paillons," or, as the French word signifies, "spangles," which are small sheets of absolutely pure gold or silver, of from thirty to fifty times the thickness of gold leaf; these are embedded in transparent enamel, or in the surface of the copper foundation, without allowing air to penetrate beneath.

The light rays, on passing through the translucent layers of enamel applied to the vase, rebound off the mirrored foil with increased brilliance and iridescence. Other parts of the vase generate the reverse effect of opacity,

an opaque enamel is floated over the relief ornament: a process difficult even for flat surfaces, and still more complicated when applied to relief ornament. Over this opaque substance, colored enamel is then added according to the design; thin, transparent glazes being mainly used to produce the quality needed. In cases when the natural color of the metal enters into the scheme, the glaze is permitted to over-run the entire subject, giving a still further tone, by increasing depth, perspective, and luster.

These light-reflective techniques, carefully juxtaposed throughout the composition to provide areas of contrasting light and shadow, provided Tiffany with a diverse palette with which to achieve the rich naturalistic effect that he sought, one heightened further by the fruit standing out in bas-relief.

Despite the enthusiasm for Tiffany's achievements, the enamel department remained small. Its staff in its formative years consisted of no more than a handful of young women: Julia Munson, Patricia Gay, and Alice Goovy (enamelers), and apprentices.[15] Output was correspondingly small, with prices ranging from $10 for a small desk item to $900 for an elaborate enameled lamp base. After 1904, there were no specific references to the department in the firm's literature. It appears that it closed as quietly as it began, probably around 1910. It was reopened in 1921 when Tiffany Furnaces, the successor to Tiffany Studios, introduced a new line of enamelware (mainly desk sets) under Patricia Gay, who had been lured back from retirement.

Shreve & Company

Shreve & Company began as a jewelry store in San Francisco in 1852 and by degrees established itself as a leading producer of hollow-ware, trophies, and souvenir spoons.[16] Around the turn of the century, presentation pieces

96 *Pitcher in the "XIV Century II" pattern, by Shreve & Company (c.1900). Silver. The lightly planished body and rim are applied with cut-out Gothic scrapwork ornamentation; the applied C-handle is similarly decorated and bears an elaborate incised monogram. 9¹/₁₆in. (23cm.) high; 3¹¹/₁₆in. (9.4cm.) diameter of base. Collection of R. A. Ellison*

became a specialty, including a silver service presented to Admiral George Dewey's flagship, *Olympia,* and a silver statue entitled *A Bear Fight,* presented in 1903 to President Theodore Roosevelt. At this time, George R. Shreve (son of one of the firm's founders) began to experiment with hand-hammered surfaces used in conjunction with cutout designs.

A pitcher in the XIV Century II pattern of around 1900 (96) is a fine example of this technique. Its Gothic ornamentation is part of a series of flat- and hollow-ware patterns introduced by Shreve at the turn of the century as "XIV Century I" and "XIV Century II." These, identified today broadly as "Shreve Strap," are the firm's most readily known designs. In the "XIV Century I" series,[17] each item is adorned with a different Gothic motif, whereas all of the pieces in the "XIV Century II" series incorporate the same studded Cross motif. The pattern later provided the inspiration for a nearly identical model, "Crusader," introduced by Newburyport silversmiths.

The cutout sections of strapwork are soldered on to the body and not riveted, as the imitation bosses make it appear. The technique shows the modern silversmith's compromise: the marriage of the medieval ironmonger's style – with an evocation of its craft techniques and archaic construction – and a time-saving method of assembly. It was a compromise forced increasingly on the late Victorian silversmith as the machine transformed his cottage industry into a commercial enterprise. The simulated bosses have decorative counterparts in other areas of the American Arts and Crafts Movement; in particular, the pegs applied to some Stickley and Greene & Greene furniture to provide a decorative accent to large paneled areas of wood. The use of such non-functional decoration, even when disguised as structural components, was, of course, contrary to the basic philosophy of the Arts and Crafts credo, but everybody bent the rules on occasion.

Shreve & Company introduced twenty basic flatware patterns designed by Joseph Birmingham, which were available either at its store or by catalogue. Catalogues were issued biennially between 1909 and 1913. Included was a wide range of Classical designs such as this "XIV Century" pattern, Louis XVI, Adam, Norman I, Napoleonic, and Windsor.[18] Designs were simple and the pieces were die-cast and given a hand-hammered finish to disguise this fact. Special emphasis was given to monograms, which became a means of adding understated ornament.

Robert Riddle Jarvie

Robert Jarvie (1865–1941) was born in Schenectady, New York, of Scottish parents and later moved to Chicago. An early interest in lighting led by 1900 to a serious part-time career as a metalworker, with emphasis on light fixtures, especially candlesticks.[19] A contemporary critic described his early progress.

Mr. Jarvie was not satisfied with the modern candlesticks he found in the shops, and following his custom of making for himself what he cannot find elsewhere, he designed and made a brass candlestick. Its success was so great that others soon followed, and Mr. Jarvie earned for himself the sobriquet of "The Candlestick-maker." Nearly all this work is of cast bronze or copper, brush polished, a process

97 *Pair of Candlesticks, designed by Robert Jarvie (1903–06).*
Cast brass, brush-polished. Each candlestick has a "bôbeche" and applied foot. 13½in. (34.3cm.) high; 5⁵⁄₁₆in. (15.1cm.) diameter of foot.
Collection of Joel Silver

which leaves the metal with a dull glow. Some pieces are cast in bronze and their unpolished surfaces are treated with acids which produce an exquisite antique finish. There is also a quaint design in spun brass: a low candlestick with a handle, quite different from the tall ones. The charm of these candlesticks is in their simplicity and purity of form. The graceful outlines and soft luster of the unembellished metal combine to produce dignity as well as beauty.[20]

Jarvie displayed two lanterns in an exhibition sponsored by the Chicago Arts and Crafts Society in 1900, two years later showing a lampshade and selection of candlesticks at the inaugural Art-Craft Exhibition at the Chicago Art Institute. The slender, fluid forms of his candlesticks set them apart from those of the imitators who quickly emerged. As orders increased, Jarvie commissioned two local foundries, the Turner Brass Works and W. B. Anderson, to execute some of his designs. In 1904 he resigned his job with the Chicago Department of Transportation, opening the Jarvie Shop in the Fine Arts Building, at 203 Michigan Avenue.[21] Soon his output included sixteen different candlestick models, in addition to lamps and miscellaneous household metalware.[22]

Jarvie divided his candlestick production between casting and spinning, the former process preferred for tall slender forms as in the pair of candlesticks of around 1903–06 (97), and the latter for a selection of shorter, trumpet-shaped sticks. It is likely that his first essays, undertaken in his own home, were spun, due to the comparative facility and cheapness of installing a lathe rather than a furnace. Copper items were most easily spun as the metal's softness and malleability are well suited to the formation of tapered or domed shapes. Brass, however, is better cast as its heavier gauge and specific gravity require continual annealing during spinning to prevent friction and the subsequent possibility of cracking.

In 1909 Jarvie moved from the Fine Arts Building to 1340 E. 47th Street, following which he made a third, and final, move in 1912 to 842 Exchange Avenue in the Union Stock Yards, where he was to remain until 1920. The move to the Stock Yards was initiated by Arthur G. Leonard, the President of the Union Stock Yard Company, whose responsibilities included the commission of trophies awarded annually to cattle breeders. Mr. Leonard thought the traditional offering of loving cups and trophies to be inappropriate and hackneyed and commissioned Jarvie to design a new and functional range of awards. Jarvie responded with a selection of gold, silver, and brass items that "were judged to be beautiful, useful, and fitted to the purposes of the people who will own them."[23]

In 1912 a trophy (98) was commissioned by the *Aero and Hydro* magazine to be offered by the Aero Club of Illinois "to encourage the development of the hydroaeroplane, or aero-hydroplane ... and at the same time to provide an annual event to encourage competition among operators of this type of flying machine."[24] The commission specified that Jarvie recreate on the trophy's lid a model of a flying boat made by the Curtiss Aeroplane Company.

A piece which received equal celebrity to the Aero Club trophy was Jarvie's Indian Motif punch bowl, presented by Charles L. Hutchinson to the Cliff Dwellers Club of Chicago, an organization of painters, musicians, and artist/craftsmen.[25]

98 Trophy, designed by Robert Jarvie (1912).
Handwrought silver. The cover is mounted with the model of a sea bi-plane; the flaring circular body has an incised band at the rim above a ribbed column and tiered square foot. 15⅜in. (39cm.) high; 10in. (25.4cm.) diameter.
Courtesy, Chicago Historical Society

144

Kalo Shops

Born in Oregon, Clara Barck Welles (1868–1965) opened the first Kalo Shop at 175 Dearborn, Chicago, in 1900, on graduation from the city's Art Institute.[26] The name Kalo came from the Greek word for beautiful. When she married George S. Welles in 1905, her initial interest in handcrafted leather and weaving shifted to metalware and jewelry. The couple set up a workshop behind their Park Ridge home, naming it the Kalo Art-Craft Community. Here Clara and a team of craftswomen created wares for the shop they had opened in the Fine Arts Building at 203 Michigan Avenue. An energetic woman known as a fair employer, teacher, and promoter of women's causes, Welles oversaw the production of a wide range of copper, brass, and silver household wares. Emphasis was placed on simple forms with lightly hammered finishes expressive of the metal. With the number of staff growing to twenty-five, Kalo Shops became the leading producer of silverware for more than three generations of Chicagoans. Welles retired in 1940, though the Shops continued to operate until 1970.

The design of a bracelet (99) by Welles at the Kalo Shops between 1900 and 1910 shows strong Danish influence. Both the chrysoprase cabochon and conventionalized leaf-and-pod motifs are closely related to Georg Jensen's interpretation of the Art Nouveau aesthetic. Kalo's link to Scandinavia was strengthened by the string of young Danish silversmiths – including Daniel P. Pederson and Yngve H. Olsson – hired by Welles in the early years of the century.

The bracelet is impressed *STERLING KALO*, indicating that it was probably made in the years 1900–10. Around 1910, the words *HAND BEATEN* were added, no doubt to impress on clients that the Shops persisted in handwrought techniques at a time when machine production was on the increase within the industry. In 1914, new marks were again introduced, including the word *CHICAGO* to mark the Shop's move from Park Ridge.[27]

The general form of a sugar and creamer (100), and their application of hardstones, dates them to the Kalo Shops' early years. At this time, Welles took special inspiration from her counterparts in the parent English Arts and Crafts Movement.

The influence of Ashbee, in particular, is unmistakable in the graceful fusion of horizontal and bulbous forms. The choice of colorful stones as a decorative accent is found in many of his Cymric and Tudric pieces for Liberty in the early years of this century.[28] The attention paid to the design of the monogram – specifically, the curved outer legs of the A and M letter, which conform to the contour of the pieces – add finesse and subtlety to the overall composition.[29]

Ashbee's influence in America was particularly profound in Chicago, where an exhibition of his jewelry and silver had been staged in the city's inaugural Arts and Crafts exhibition in 1898 at the Art Institute. Two years later, during his tour of the U.S.A., Ashbee's lecture at the Institute generated further publicity for his Guild of Handicraft and its Arts and Crafts ideals.

A silver and abalone tray, probably designed by Welles (101), may be one of the last of Kalo's more decorated pieces. The lobed shape of a pitcher

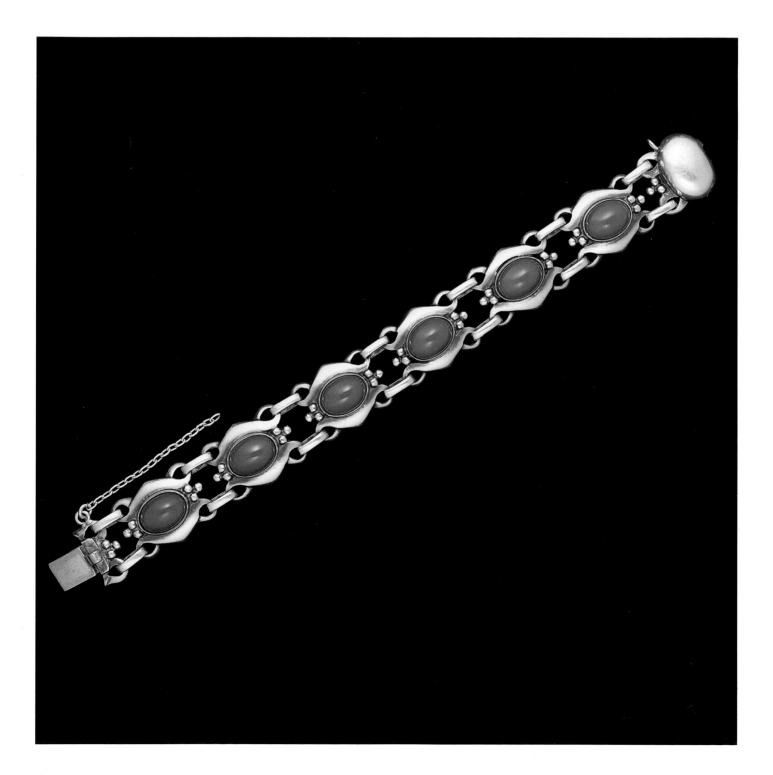

Opposite above

100 Sugar and Creamer, designed by Clara B. Welles, the Kalo Shops (1905–10). Silver and jade. Each is spherical, with an angled C-handle set on the top with a jade cabochon, the obverse chased in relief with the conjoined monogram "AMS." Creamer: 2⅛in. (5.4cm.) high; 4¾in. (12.1cm.) diameter. Sugar: 2⅛in. (5.4cm.) high; 4⅝in. (11.8cm.) diameter.
Courtesy, Chicago Historical Society

Opposite below

101 (Left) Pitcher, by the Lebolt Company (probably 1923). Silver. Tapering, with a flaring rim and spout, C-handle, and lightly hammered finish. 8⅝in. (21.9cm.) high; 4¾in. (12cm.) diameter of foot.
Collection of Gabriela Brown, New York
(Right above) Pitcher, probably designed by Clara B. Welles, the Kalo Shops (1914–20). Silver. The serpentine rim has a banded edge; the body has 6 leaf-form lobes and is applied with a C-handle. 9¼in. (23.5cm.) high; 4¹³⁄₁₆in. (12.2cm.) diameter of base.
Private Collection
(Right below) Tray, probably designed by Clara B. Welles, the Kalo Shops (1910–14). Silver and abalone. With a raised border and recessed center; decorated with a bezel-set abalone cabochon. 7½in. (19cm.) long; 4⅝in. (11.7cm.) wide.
Collection of Gabriela Brown, New York

Below left

102 Brooch, designed and executed by A. Fogliata at the Hull-House Shops (c.1905). Gold and opals. The gold mount is cast at the top with flowers inset with opal centers and framing an oblong opal. 6 opal cabochons are suspended at the bottom from linked gold chains. 2¾in. (7cm.) high.
Courtesy, Chicago Historical Society

Below right

103 Pendant, designed and executed by A. Fogliata at the Hull-House Shops (c.1905). Gold, opals, and topaz. Designed as a Belle Epoque maiden playing a flute in a forest inset at the top with topaz blooms. 3 opal drops are suspended from the bottom. 2¾in. (7cm.) high; 1⅜in. (3.5cm.) wide.
Courtesy, Chicago Historical Society

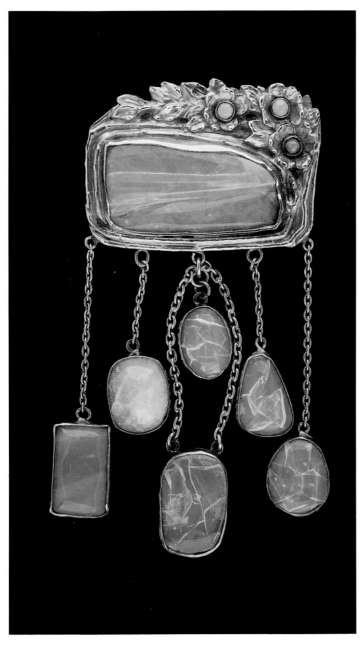

(101), also attributed to Welles, corresponds to a shift of style adopted by the Kalo Shops in the 1910–20 period away from ornamentation, such as applied hardstones and paneling, to a pure and unbroken roundness of form.

A. Fogliata: Hull House Shops

Little is known of Fogliata, the designer of a brooch of gold and opals (102) of *c.* 1905 and a pendant of gold, opals, and topaz (103) of the same period, beyond that he was associated as a metalworker and jeweler with the Hull-House Shops in Chicago in the early years of this century.

The Hull-House Shops, at 800 South Halsted Street, became a center for craft-related activities.[30] Its facilities included a shop, lecture program, symposia, and workshop classes from around 1898 to 1940. In the years 1903–11, it appears that Fogliata and Isadore Friedman were responsible primarily for the execution in metal and enamels of the designs of Frank Hazenplug, a resident designer.

The brooch was made for Mrs. Frances M. Glessner.[31] Its incorporation of inexpensive opals, as well as its floral theme, recall the work of several French Art Nouveau jewelers at the time, especially René Lalique, Georges Fouquet, and Lucien Gaillard. The mid-nineteenth century jeweler's preoccupation with precious stones had yielded by 1900 to an acceptance of inexpensive materials such as horn, ivory, freshwater pearls, enamel, abalone, and even molded glass. The fire opals in this brooch fall into this category, their internal brilliance providing a rich counterpoint to the gold mount, despite their relative cheapness.

Lebolt Company

The classical simplicity and understated elegance of a silver pitcher (101) designed probably in 1923 is characteristic of Lebolt's wares. The monogram is a popular feature, by which the firm could introduce an unobtrusive decorative accent to the lightly hammered surface of the piece.

The retail jewelry firm of Lebolt & Company was established in 1899 by J. Myer H. Lebolt at 167 South State Street, Chicago,[32] and around 1912 a metalshop was added. Lebolt developed a series of distinctive hand-hammered tea and coffee services and flatware patterns to supplement the firm's jewelry. By the 1920s roughly three dozen patterns were in production, in addition to a large volume of custom work. Styles ranged from the traditional – for example, Gothic, Louis XVI, and Georgian – to a selection of unadorned Arts and Crafts pieces heightened only with a lightly hammered surface finish. A staff of roughly twenty-five designers and artisans – silver and goldsmiths, polishers, chasers, stone-cutters and setters – were retained in the workshop, which from 1907 to 1925 was situated in a building adjacent to the Lebolt shop in the Palmer House at 101 South State Street. A second retail outlet was opened in Paris around 1910, and a third on Fifth Avenue, New York, in 1924. The metalshop closed during World War II, because of metal rationing. At present the firm has five Chicago outlets and two in Milwaukee.

4 Lighting and Windows

The Arts and Crafts light fixture stood in direct contrast to the host of Tiffany and Tiffany-style lamps found in many American homes at the turn of the century. First, it was subdued and monochromatic, unlike the kaleidoscopic floral designs on Art Nouveau leaded glass shades. Even when more than one color was used, as in the geometric lamps and windows of Frank Lloyd Wright and Dard Hunter, colors were complementary and muted, in keeping with the warm brown palette of an interior furnished in wood and leather. Mica, which has a soft golden translucency, became a popular choice for Arts and Crafts lamp makers such as Van Erp and the Roycrofters.

Lamp forms were similarly simple: proportion and workmanship became the medium's standard-bearers. To emphasize the manual dexterity required in their creation, special attention was paid by lamp makers to the finish on these fixtures. Surfaces were embellished by hammering or planishing, a proud measure of the craftsman's skills. Dirk Van Erp emerged as a foremost designer of Arts and Crafts lamps.

Frank Lloyd Wright

As in the case of his furniture designs, Wright's use of windows and lighting fixtures was almost invariably connected with specific houses. In 1900, for example, he was engaged in the building of a residence in Kankakee, Illinois, for his enthusiastic client B. Harley Bradley.[1] The house, called "Glenlloyd," was an ambitious project, one in which every detail was custom-made, including draperies, carpets, light fixtures, and furniture. The design of the living room windows became an integral part of the overall plan. Certain arched details, accentuated in the windows by the use of broad zinc cames, echo the angle of the house's stepped roof. No documentation survives to explain Wright's choice of the Indian motif on this panel (104), but his interest in local tribes had been apparent during the years he was growing up in Wisconsin, and in later years he became a collector of Indian artifacts. He also incorporated Indian bronzes in his interiors.

For the Dana house in Springfield, he designed a glass table lamp (105), of which variations occur within the house.[2] The house contains both the largest and finest selection of Wright's glass.[3] The lamp reflects his long-standing infatuation with the art and architecture of Japan, which he had developed at an early age by collecting Japanese prints. Its form evolves from the flat overhanging shape of the country's pagoda roofs and parasols.[4] It was executed c. 1903 by the Linden Glass Company in Chicago.[5]

In his essay "In the Cause of Architecture," which appeared in *Architectural Record* in July 1928, Wright looked back at his attempt in his

104 *Ceiling Fixture, designed by Frank Lloyd Wright for the B. Harley Bradley house, Kankakee, Illinois (c.1900). Glass with zinc cames. Decorated with a geometric pattern incorporating a central Indian motif, in opalescent amber, gold, white, and pale green glass. Sometimes referred to as a skylight, this panel was in fact installed in a recess in the dining room ceiling and lit artificially. This is why it was executed in opalescent glass. 33½in. (85cm.) high; 16½in. (42cm.) wide. Private Collection*

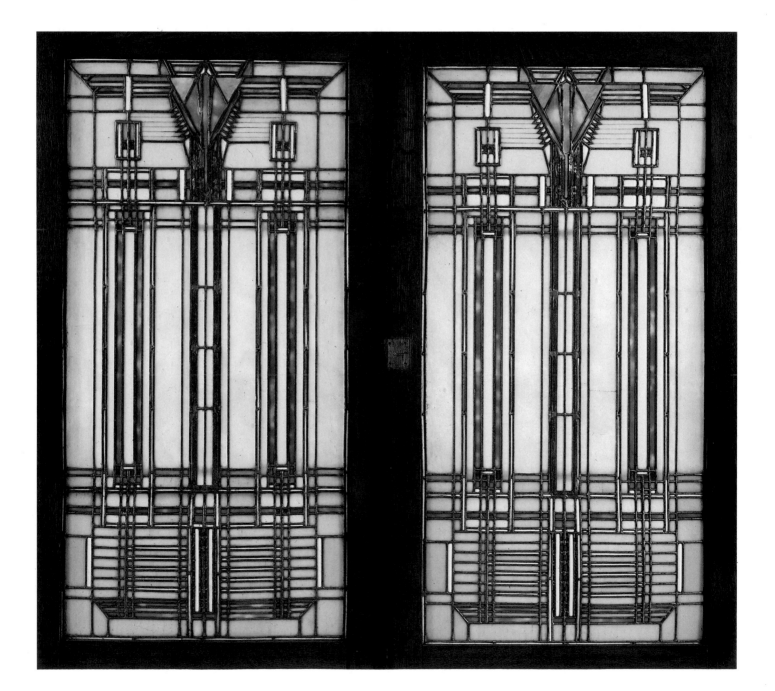

105 Table Lamp, designed by Frank Lloyd Wright for the Dana house, Springfield, Illinois, executed by the Linden Glass Company, Chicago (c.1903).
Paneled glass, with electroplated gilt zinc cames, on a brass base. The shallow 16-sided shade is decorated with leaded green and purple panels of glass alternating with unleaded amber panels. It is raised on twin brass columns suspending between them a panel of iridescent green glass. The base consists of 4 indented cubes. 23in. (58.4cm.) high; 26in. (66cm.) diameter of shade. The Dana-Thomas House. The Illinois Historic Preservation Agency. Photo Photographic Services Corporation

first Prairie School homes to integrate freestanding lamps such as this into his architectural schemes. He wrote,

Then, too, there is the lighting fixture, made a part of the building. No longer an appliance nor even an appurtenance, but really architecture. This is a new field. I touched it early in my work and can see limitless possibilities of beauty in this one feature of the use of glass ... it will soon be a disgrace to an architect to have left anything of a physical nature whatsoever in his building unassimilated in his design as a whole.[6]

The Linden Glass Company also executed a pair of reception hall doors with sumac blossoms for the Dana house (107). Indeed, this company, established in 1890, produced most of Wright's glass windows and chandeliers; proud of its association with Wright, the company used the Dana house sumac door panels to advertise its work in contemporary architectural magazines.

In 1903 Wright started drawing up plans for a residence in Buffalo commissioned by Darwin Martin, a brother of William Martin who lived in an Oak Park house designed by Wright. Unrestricted by a budget, Wright indulged his most extravagant ideas about the fittings and fixtures appropriate to a Prairie School structure, and was free to design all aspects of the interior. The geometric pattern of this living room window (106) was not characteristic of Wright's designs for glass, which were usually composed of conventionalized plant forms, such as the "Tree of Life" examples elsewhere in the same house.[7]

The composition here is understated, its quiet symmetry enlivened only by the sparkle of the iridescent panels interspersed evenly throughout the composition. This eye-catching effect recalls a later statement by Wright on his windows, "I have used opalescent, opaque, white and gold in the geometrical groups of spots fixed in the clear glass. I have used, preferably, clear primary colors, like the German flashed glass, to get decorative effects, believing the clear emphasis of the primitive color interferes less with the function of the window and adds a higher architectural note to the effect of light itself."[8] The iridescent colored glass incorporated in the Martin house windows (and elsewhere in Wright commissions) by the Linden Glass Company, was imported from Germany. Bins of it were compiled from which Wright could make his selection. In *Frank Lloyd Wright to 1910* (1958), Grant Carpenter Mason describes the Darwin Martin house, "with its use of casement windows and brickwork both outside and in," as "the most striking example to date of that determination of Wright's to demolish the hard-and-fast distinction between the exterior and interior of a house."[9]

Among Wright's most famous windows are those he designed for the Avery Coonley Playhouse in Riverside, Illinois. Wright had designed a spectacular sprawling residence for the wealthy Coonley family in 1907–08, and, several years later, Mrs. Coonley commissioned him to build a playhouse/school on the same six-acre property overlooking the Desplaines River.[10] She wanted a private building in which to educate her nine-year-old daughter and a few neighbors' children by the progressive methods advanced by John Dewey at the University of Chicago. Wright undertook the commission immediately after his return from Europe in 1911. Unlike anything he had done previously, the interior of the playhouse was

106 Window, designed by Frank Lloyd Wright for the living room of the Darwin D. Martin house at 125 Jewett Parkway, Buffalo, New York, executed by the Linden Glass Company, Chicago (c.1904).
Glass with zinc cames. The window, set in a wooden frame, consists of 7 horizontal grids of leaded glass in a symmetrical geometric pattern, in yellow, gold, and brown glass. Some panels have a surface iridescence. 42in. (106.7cm.) high; 22½in. (57.2cm.) wide.
Private Collection, Courtesy of the Jordan-Volpe Gallery, New York

107 Pair of Reception Hall Doors, designed by Frank Lloyd Wright for the Dana house, Springfield, Illinois, executed by the Linden Glass Company, Chicago (c.1903).
Paneled glass with zinc cames. Glazed with slightly differing abstract geometric designs of pendant trellised sumac blossoms in iridescent amber and yellow tones on a clear ground. Each panel: 60¾in. (154.3cm.) high; 19¾in. (50.2cm.) wide.
The Dana-Thomas House. The Illinois Historic Preservation Agency. Photo Photographic Services Corporation

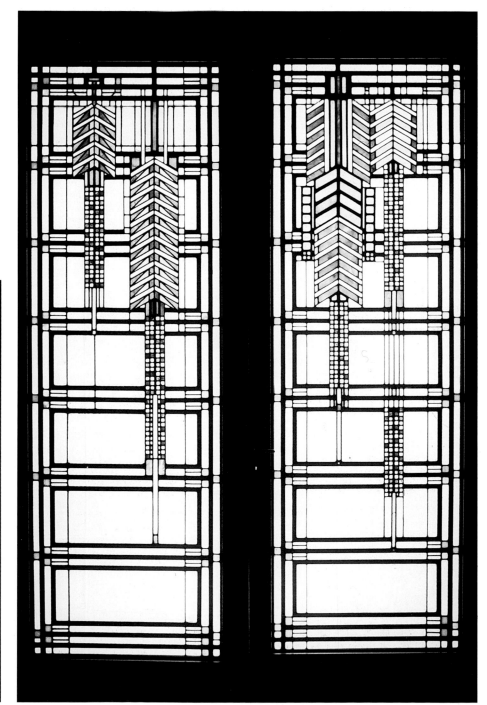

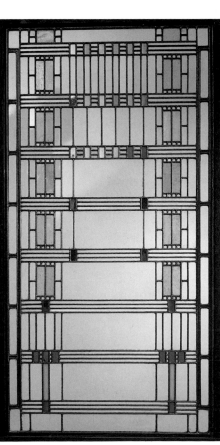

108   Window, designed by Frank Lloyd
Wright for the Avery Coonley Playhouse,
Riverside, Illinois, executed by the Linden
Glass Company, Chicago (1912).
Glass panels with zinc cames. Designed as an
abstract composition including balloons, flags,
and confetti in opaque primary colors on a
clear ground. 86¼in. (219cm.) high; 28in.
(71.1cm.) wide.
Collection of The Metropolitan Museum of
Art, New York. Purchase, Edgar J. Kaufman
Foundation and Edward C. Moore, Jr., Gifts
1967

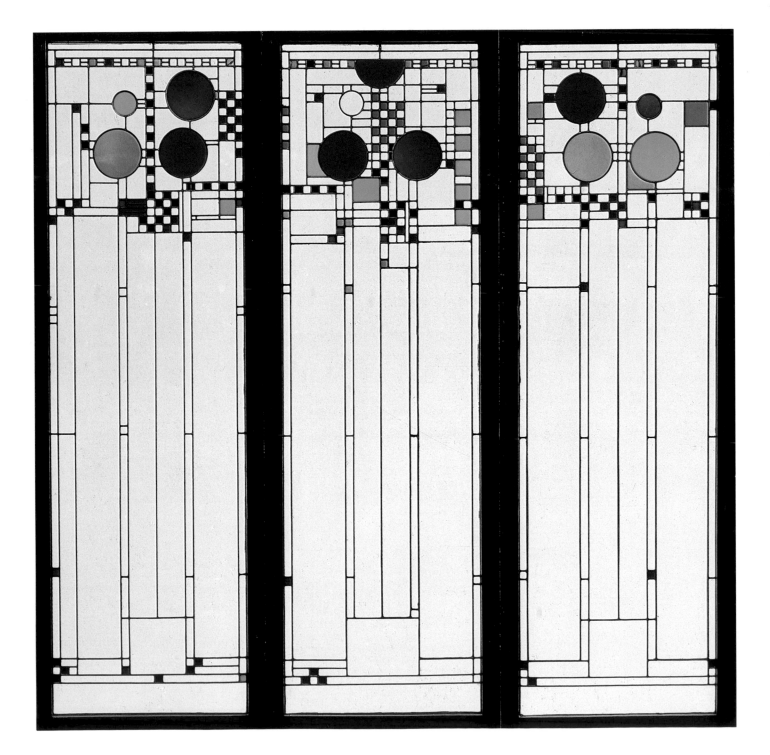

dominated by the windows (108), their bright primary colors providing a light and playful ambience well suited to a classroom setting. The windows suggest an affinity with contemporary European abstract painters, such as Francis Picabia, Robert Delaunay, and Frank Kupka, whose work Wright probably saw during his trip. The effect clearly pleased him, for he used a variation of colored overlapping circles in the mural he made for the Midway Gardens in 1913 and again to decorate his porcelain tableware for the Imperial Hotel in Tokyo.

Tiffany and Grueby

In today's market, the shade in a Tiffany/Grueby lamp has often been assumed to be the more valuable, but in the case of a fish-scale model created sometime between 1898 and 1902 (109), the base is the more important, reminding us of the respect afforded Grueby in his own time.[11] A critic, in the 12 May 1900 issue of *The Chicago Illinois Post*, drew attention to this in his review of the Exposition Universelle,

> Tiffany glass and Grueby pottery occupy prominent and neighboring positions at the Paris Exposition and are meeting with much success there. In the very first week, when exhibits were hardly in order and no one expected to sell goods, $365 worth of dull green pottery was sold. Most of the pieces selected were the large, ambitious ones, which are rarely salable in America. The managers of the Grueby pottery feel encouraged to experiment in new lines, and it has proved that Europeans are more ready than ourselves to accept artistic wares without waiting for the sanction of time and fashion.

Another type of Grueby base for a Tiffany vine border shade, designed between 1900 and 1905 (110), has a broad mouth, and was often used by American lamp manufacturers at the turn of the century to house a fuel canister. Aside from Tiffany, this kind of base was used by Bigelow, Kennard, & Co., and Duffner & Kimberly.

Grueby's subtle monochromatic glazes were found to be an admirable complement to the muted palette of the leaded glass shades, especially those with geometric patterns, of that period.[12] It was anticipated in 1906 that Tiffany Studios would phase out its use of Grueby bases and replace them with its own newly introduced range of ceramic wares; but this did not occur, as the firm was at the time in the process of converting its combustion light fixtures to electricity. This eliminated the need for bases to house fuel canisters. The result was a sharp decrease in the use of Grueby wares by lamp manufacturers.

Roycroft

Around 1905, Dard Hunter designed and executed a table lamp of American white oak and leaded glass (111) for the dining room of Emerson Hall, which was an ancillary hostelry one and a half blocks from the Roycroft Inn on South Grove Street, East Aurora, New York. It was built in 1905–06; a contemporary postcard shows settings of two and three lamps on dining tables beneath matching chandeliers (now gone).[13]

109   Table Lamp, Tiffany Studios (shade)
and the Grueby Faience Company (base)
(1898–1902).
Leaded glass and ceramics. Shade: domed,
decorated with radiating bands of fish scales
in white-mottled emerald green glass. 26in.
(66cm.) diameter. Base: modeled (probably
from a design by George Prentiss Kendrick)
with twin bands of 5 leaves each, the curled
leaf tips in high relief. Decorated in a mat
dark green glaze. 33⅝in. (85.4cm.) height to
top of lampshade.
The Jordan-Volpe Gallery, New York

Below

111   Table Lamp, *designed and executed by Dard Hunter at the Roycroft Shops (1905–06).*
American white oak and leaded glass, with copper mounts. The shade is of squared conical form, each side with an upper triangular opalescent white panel on a glazed emerald ground; the oak frame is supported by 4 pairs of hand-wrought copper mounts; the square base is raised on a stepped oak plinth. 18^{11}/$_{16}$in. (47.5cm.) diameter of shade; 25^3/$_4$in. (65.4cm.) high.
Private Collection

Opposite above

112   Chandelier, *designed and executed by Dard Hunter, with copper mounts by Karl Kipp, at the Roycroft Shops (c.1906). Designed for the Roycroft Inn. The chandelier consists of 5 lantern-formed shades, the central shade with 3 panels depicting the professions of book printing, architecture, and sculpture, and the fourth panel matching the 4 flanking shades. 12in. (30.4cm.) diameter of central shade; 30^1/$_2$in. (77.4cm.) height from bottom of central shade to the ceiling; 26in. (66cm.) diameter of entire chandelier.*
Kitty Turgeon – Robert Rust, The Roycroft Inn and Shops, East Aurora, New York.
Photo Eric Demme

Opposite below

113   Window, *designed and executed by Dard Hunter at the Roycroft Shops (c.1906). Designed for the Roycroft Inn, with a central formalized rose and leaf motif on a glazed rectangular clear glass ground. 60^1/$_2$in. (153.6cm.) high; 32in. (81.3cm.) wide.*
Kitty Turgeon – Robert Rust, The Roycroft Inn and Shops, East Aurora, New York.
Photo Eric Demme

Hunter's son records that most of the glass used by the Roycrofters was purchased from the Opalescent Glass Works in Kokomo, Indiana. A sample shipment was sent in December, 1905, for lampshade production. By March of the following year roughly 200lb of assorted colors had been received, followed by a similar shipment two years later.[14] The glass's deep mottle can easily be mistaken for the same effect produced by Tiffany Studios in some of its most famous varieties of textured and diochroic glass.

Hunter created several variations of this lampshade, some of which are visible in photographs taken in both the Inn and Elbert Hubbard's office.[15] The most elaborate of them, in which landscape, heraldic, and aquatic themes on the shades were continued in leaded panels set in the base, resemble late nineteenth-century British and European pictorial windows, and are uncharacteristically Victorian in feeling for Roycroft.[16]

Hunter obtained a rudimentary knowledge of how to work in stained glass through the foreign craft publications available at Roycroft. In 1904, Hubbard sent him on a two-months comprehensive training course at the J. & R. Lamb Studio in New York City. By early 1906 Hunter was in charge of all stained glass production at Roycroft, a role he maintained, among his other responsibilties, for the remaining five years he was there.[17]

His chandelier of c. 1906 for the Music Room in the Roycroft Inn (112) was transferred in the 1920s to the front porch, where it remained for nearly thirty years. It was then brought back into the Inn and installed in the vestibule near the main entrance, where it hangs today, the most identifiable and important object which has survived from the building's earliest years. Its three central panels depict the professions of book printing, architecture, and sculpture.[18]

Among other leaded-glass light fixtures Hunter designed for the Inn before his departure in 1910 were wall sconces with squared geometric patterns, and a floor lamp decorated with a band of dragonflies similar to the well-known model of Tiffany Studios. Around 1906 he also created a set of windows (113) to replace an earlier set, which he had smashed out in a fit of despair over their pastel listlessness. The design of the windows that still exist draws directly on the conventionalized rose motif developed by the Glasgow School – in particular by Charles Rennie Mackintosh – and later further popularized by the Vienna Secession. Hunter incorporated the angular Scottish flower and leaf into a wide range of his Roycroft designs, such as covers for *The Fra* and borders for Hubbard's motto cards and placards, even before his 1908 visit to Vienna to study at the Kunstgewerbeschule. Hunter acknowledged readily the Viennese influence in his leaded glass fixtures.[19]

Greene and Greene

On the West Coast during the first decade of the twentieth century the architectural firm of Greene & Greene created a number of light fixtures and windows for specific houses. The ceiling fixture of 1907 (114) for the living room of the Freeman A. Ford house in Pasadena, California, is generally considered by historians of the firm to be their finest design in this medium. Its large size, delicate Japanese-inspired decoration, and selection

114 *Ceiling Fixture, designed by Greene and Greene for the living room of the Freeman A. Ford house, Pasadena, California, executed by the Sturdy-Lange Studios, Los Angeles (1907).*
Mahogany, ebony, iron, and leaded glass. With gently bowed sides, decorated with bird-like motifs and clouds in iridescent and lightly mottled translucent amber and gold glass, with a central band in streaked beige glass. The mahogany mount has ebony pegs and is attached to the ceiling mount (replaced) with iron straps. 45¼in. (115cm.) high; 41¹³⁄₁₆in. (104.7cm.) wide (excluding ceiling mount); 15³⁄₈in. (39.1cm.) high (excluding ceiling mount).
Collection of James and Janeen Marrin

of subtle glass tones, set it apart from the firm's other commissions. Ford, who was vice-president of the Pasadena Ice Company, commissioned Greene and Greene to design a residence for him at 215 S. Grand Avenue. It appears that Ford had been exposed to their work some years before at the time the brothers were commissioned by S. Hazard Hallsted to design an early building for the Pasadena Ice Company. The Greenes worked on the Ford house at the time when they were exploring the relationships between large structures and their sites through emphasis of the horizontal line.

Charles Sumner Greene designed in 1908–09 a pair of leaded glass doors (115) for the entrance to the Gamble house in Pasadena. One of the dominant features of the house, it consists of a central door flanked by a pair of narrower screened doors beneath an upper row of transoms. Greene's design, which extends into all the panels, depicts a gnarled California oak.

The entrance was assembled by the Sturdy-Lange Studios in Los Angeles, under the direction of Emil Lange, who had worked for some years at Tiffany Studios before moving to California. He is reported to have arrived on the West Coast with a large inventory of Tiffany glass; and examination of this entrance reveals varieties of glass which, in both their surface iridescence and translucency, appear to have been made by Tiffany. There is no evidence to substantiate whether this glass was specially ordered from Tiffany or was obtained by Lange through unauthorized means.

Dirk Van Erp

Two table lamps of copper and mica (116, 117) were designed and executed by Dirk Van Erp in San Francisco around 1910. Van Erp used their structural elements – specifically, rivets – in the same way that Arts and Crafts furniture makers used tenons and pegs. The rivets' uneven chamfered finish enhances the lamps' handwrought image, in open defiance of the encroaching machine. Unlike William Morris, who never entirely rejected the machine, or Stickley and Hubbard, who similarly saw it as a legitimate aid to, or preparation for, handwork, Van Erp took the work ethic of the Middle Ages quite literally, performing every aspect of an item's creation manually. When his son William bought an electric drill in order to expedite production, Van Erp admonished him with these words: "When you make a thing by hand, you make it by hand."[20]

Mica is fundamentally crystalline in structure, with the crystals arranged in layers, so it is easily sliced to produce the sheets used in early Arts and Crafts lampshades. Strong and pliant, these sheets provide a warm translucent glow when viewed by transmitted light. It is also non-inflammable (its primary use today is for insulation), which added to its suitability for lampshades. Mica ranges in transparency from a completely clear variety to examples in yellow and amber with air inclusions, cross-crystallization, small tears, and stains (the latter are inorganic: finely dispersed iron oxides which cause red and black stains and spots). Van Erp was drawn to mica for its incandescence in the same way that Tiffany and the Viennese designer, Gustav Gurschner, used nautilus and *Turbo Marmoratus* shells in their lamps. The word "isinglass" is sometimes used to describe Arts and Crafts mica shades.

116   *Table Lamp, designed and executed by*
Dirk Van Erp (c.1910).
Copper and stained mica. The conical shade
has 4 vertical leaf-form straps riveted to the
top cap and lower rim, enclosing curved and
stained mica panels, supported by 4 arms
attached to the ovoid base. 19in. (48.2cm.)
high; 19¾in. (50.2cm.) diameter of shade.
Collection of Robb Carr

117   *Table Lamp, designed and executed by Dirk Van Erp (c. 1910).*
Copper and stained mica. The conical shade has 4 curved mica panels within patinated copper straps riveted to the cap and lower rim. The squat hand-hammered base is applied at the top with 4 riveted and curved arms. 20½in. (52cm.) high; 24⅜in. (61.9cm.) diameter of shade.
Private Collection

Below left

118 *"Chinese Globular Bottle" Table Lamp, Vase-Kraft model no. 23, the Fulper Pottery Company (1910–14). Ceramics and glass. Decorated in a green-brown flambé glaze. The shade is inset with a band of 6 oblong amber-colored glass jewels; the spherical base has a matching glaze and is applied at the shoulder with twin openwork lug handles. 18½in. (47cm.) high; 18in. (45.7cm.) diameter of shade. Collection of R. A. Ellison*

Below right

119 *"Flowing Base Mushroom" Table Lamp, Vase-Kraft model no. 6a, the Fulper Pottery Company (1911–18). Ceramics and glass. In a cucumber green mat glaze with dark gray mottling and traces of crystalline formations. The shade is inset with panels of opalescent red and green leaded glass in a repeating design of heart-shaped flowers amid stylized foliage. 18in. (45.7cm.) high; 13in. (33cm.) diameter of shade. Collection of the Virginia Museum of Fine Arts, Richmond, Virginia. Gift of Sydney and Frances Lewis*

120 *Candlestick, designed and executed by Charles Rohlfs (1901).*
Oak and copper. Of medieval form. The candle is secured within an adjustable mount beneath a conical snuffer suspended from a similar adjustable ratchet. The T-shaped oak base has carved scroll motifs. 28in. (71.1cm.) high.
Collection of P. G. Pugsley & Sons Antiques, San Francisco, California. Photo Robert Reiter

The Fulper Pottery Company

The Fulper Pottery Company in Flemington, New Jersey, introduced a series of Vase-Kraft ceramic ware – vases, lamps, desk and smoking accessories, and so forth – at Christmas 1910. A photograph of the "Chinese Globular Bottle" lamp (118) appears in an undated Vase-Kraft catalogue (probably 1914) at a price of $35. An earlier example – most likely the prototype, which varies in the absence of a circular foot on the base and in the incorporation of a shorter neck – was included by the firm in an exhibition of new wares in New York in 1911.[21] The lamp takes its name from the shape of the base, which resembles the traditional Chinese bottle vase, and was evidently discontinued by early 1915.

The "Flowing Base Mushroom" table lamp (119) was illustrated in two of Fulper's early undated Vase-Kraft catalogues at a price of $35. It was also included in two later Vase-Kraft catalogues (probably 1916–18) at a price of $75. It last appeared in 1918, when it was described only as a "Two Light Lamp."

Fulper's promotional literature claimed that its Vase-Kraft lamps were unique in using ceramic for both base and shade. Ceramic lamp bases were common in the American decorative arts at the turn of the century – Grueby, Rookwood, and the Tiffany Studios manufactured ceramic bases to support glass shades – but no other company had introduced a ceramic shade. It now appears that the reasons for this were partly technical: not only did the clay become brittle (and therefore fragile) when exposed over a period of time to the heat of electric bulbs, but the incorporation of glass panels confronted the additional problem that glass and clay have different expansion coefficients. The resulting friction frequently cracked the glass panels, which explains the shortage of Vase-Kraft lamps today. Their rarity also arises from the fact that the firm began to phase out complex, labor-intensive product lines, such as the glass-inset lamp series, during World War I because of the shortage of available skilled manpower.

Charles Rohlfs

Charles Rohlfs's quaint candlestick model of 1901 (120) takes its design directly from the chandler's craft of the Middle Ages. The cumbersome snuffer device and mount, the latter having to be adjustable downwards to secure the candle as it burned, would have required as much supervision at the turn of the century as it had for a millennium. It can be assumed therefore that Rohlfs's design here was intended as purely decorative.

5 *Miscellaneous*

erhaps no other discipline within the American Arts and Crafts Movement adhered with such tenacity to medieval techniques as bookbinding, which took its immediate inspiration from the Kelmscott Press established by William Morris near London. Both in their selection of hand tools and presses, and use of illuminating, the Arts and Crafts bookbinder and illustrator stuck rigidly to the past traditions, even at the Roycroft Shops, where large editions were frequently produced. An extensive cottage industry of bookbinding hobbyists similarly developed, primarily on the East Coast.

In American carpet production, weaving remained a guild-type industry until well into the 1930s. At the turn of the century designers often had to seek out rural craft communities for execution of their hand-knotted examples.

Roycroft

The Roycroft Printing Shop was established in East Aurora, New York, in 1895, shortly after Elbert Hubbard's visit to William Morris's artisan colony in Hammersmith, and specifically to Morris's Kelmscott Press. "Roycroft" was both a translation of "King's Craft," and the surname of Thomas and Samuel Roycroft, two noted early English printers.

The first Roycroft book, *The Song of Songs: Which Is Solomon's*, was dated 20 January 1896. Six months earlier, Hubbard had launched the first Roycroft magazine, *The Philistine*, which continued in publication until Hubbard's death on the *Lusitania* in 1915.

In 1900 Roycroft published *The Last Ride* by Robert Browning, designed by Samuel Warner and containing ten illuminated plates by Lucy Edwards, of which the page shown here (121) is Plate IX. All the plates have a somewhat ethereal and supernatural look, recalling both the Pre-Raphaelite canvases and the Art Nouveau bronze figures of the period. The hallucinating stare of the lyre-playing maiden on this plate seems also to echo the tales of Edgar Allan Poe, which enraptured the same generation of readers.

As Jean-François Vilain has noted, the designs for *The Last Ride* were copied from illustrations done by Henri Coruchet for Octave Uzanne's book *Voyage autour de sa chambre*, published in 1896 by H. Floury in Paris.[1]

Lucy Edwards was one of the young women trained in hand-illuminating by Warner, who joined Hubbard in 1898 to oversee this aspect of book production at the Roycroft Shops. The leather shop at Roycroft, which grew out of the bindery, was headed by Frederick (Fritz) C. Kranz (1879–1919). Kranz came from Germany and had spent several years working for Rump and Sons, a Philadelphia leather goods firm, before joining Roycroft in 1903. He brought with him an affinity for the European Art Nouveau

121   Illuminated Page from "The Last
Ride" by Robert Browning, designed by
Samuel Warner and hand-illuminated by
Lucy Edwards, the Roycroft Studios (1900).
Bound in suede, no. 368 of an edition of 940.
8in. (20.3cm.) high; 6¼in. (15.9cm.) wide.
Collection of Tod M. Volpe

122   "Respectability," tooled leather
bookbinding, designed by Frederick C. Kranz,
the Roycroft Studios (1905).
English calf. 8in. (20.3cm.) high; 6¼in.
(15.9cm.) wide.
Collection of Tod M. Volpe

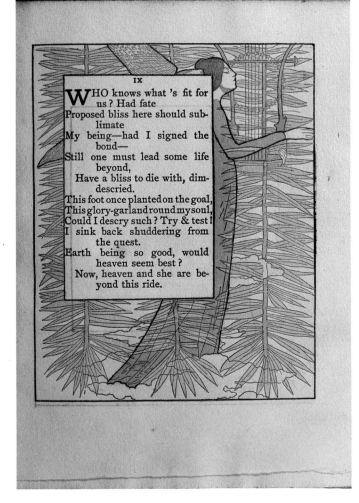

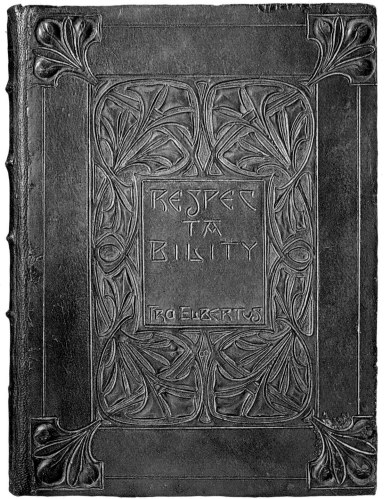

esthetic, which he applied to many of the bindings modeled by the women in the Roycroft leather shop. His design for *Respectability* (122) is typical of his formalized floral designs in which the title is contained within a compact symmetrical leaf border. Several examples of this binding have survived, each with slight hand-tooling differences. The number of this edition appears to have been roughly twenty.

Kranz's work is invariably unsigned, but he is also thought to be the designer of the binding for *Contemplations*, which has a spirited Art Nouveau floral image on its cover that is representative of his best work.

Both *Contemplations* and *Respectability* were works by Hubbard himself. *Respectability – Its Rise and Remedy* was a handsome work printed on handmade paper in two colors, with special initials, ends of Morris marbled paper, and cut-leather binding, at a price of $10. The model was illustrated in the *Roycroft Catalogue* (1912), and in *Handmade at the Roycroft Shops East Aurora New York* (1916). The book was one of several Hubbard works, including *Chicago Tongue* and *Get Out or Get in Line*, that poked fun at bourgeois standards. It was described in Roycroft literature as a book "in which Elbert Hubbard had something to say of respectability – its rise and remedy. A gently satirical book, yet kindly and broadminded withal." Hubbard claimed that it was inspired by Veblen's *A Theory of the Leisure Class* and William Morris's *News from Nowhere*.

In addition to bindings, the Roycroft leather shop generated a wide range of hand-tooled goods, such as wallets, bookends, manicure cases, tie cases, sachets, and photograph frames, which were labeled as "conveniences."[2] Kranz left Roycroft around 1915 to form his own Cordova Shops in Buffalo, which specialized in a similar range of fine modeled leather goods.

The designer of the binding (124) for *The Law of Love* (1905) is unrecorded, though its traditional European form of decoration suggests that it was executed under the supervision of Louis H. Kinder, head of the bindery. Kinder was one of the first master craftsmen whom Hubbard invited to East Aurora. An expert bookbinder and leatherworker trained in Leipzig, Kinder established the Roycroft bookbindery as an adjunct to the printshop. His students included Charles W. Youngers, Frederick Kranz, and Peter Franck.[3]

Hubbard's epigrams were collected in an anthology, *The Motto Book*, of 1909 (123), designed by Dard Hunter. The book also included selections from Solomon, Ruskin, Shakespeare, and Franklin. It was a lighthearted venture, a counterpoint to the more serious literary and proselytizing works generated by the Roycroft Printshop.

The cover's Japanese-inspired, Aesthetic Movement composition, and its selection of pastel colors, show a close similarity to other examples of Hunter's work. Most of the mottos included in the catalogue, many within delicate floral borders, were reproductions from the back cover of *The Philistine*. Other Roycroft artists whose work appears in *The Motto Book* are Jerome Connor, John Comstock, Theodore Neuhuys, Burt Barnes, Raymond Nott, and C. Foote.

Hubbard's epigrams were to be found not only in Roycroft's books, but also on two doors in the Roycroft Inn: the main entrance to the Philanestery (Meeting Place of Friends), and the entrance to the Music Salon (125). The

123 *"The Motto Book," catalogue designed by Dard Hunter, the Roycroft Studios (1909). Hand-made paper; block-printed in colors, saddlestitched, and unpaginated, with artist's conjoined signature, lower right. 8in. (20.3cm.) high; 6⅛in. (15.5cm.) wide. Collection of Tod M. Volpe*

124 *"The Law of Love," bookbinding, executed under the supervision of Louis H. Kinder, the Roycroft Studios (1905). ¾ bound red levant with a repeating gold-blocked floral design, no. 6 of an edition of 106 on Japan Vellum. 7⅞in. (20cm.) high; 6in. (15.2cm.) wide. Collection of Tod M. Volpe*

125 *Entrance Door, executed by the Roycroft Furniture Shop for the entrance to the Music Salon in the Roycroft Inn (c.1900). Oak and copper. Carved and painted in black with the lettering "The love you liberate in your work is the love you keep"; applied with a copper key escutcheon and 2 broad hand-wrought copper strap hinges. 90½in. (230cm.) high; 53¾in. (136.5cm.) wide. Kitty Turgeon – Robert Rust, The Roycroft Inn and Shops, East Aurora, New York. Photo Eric Demme*

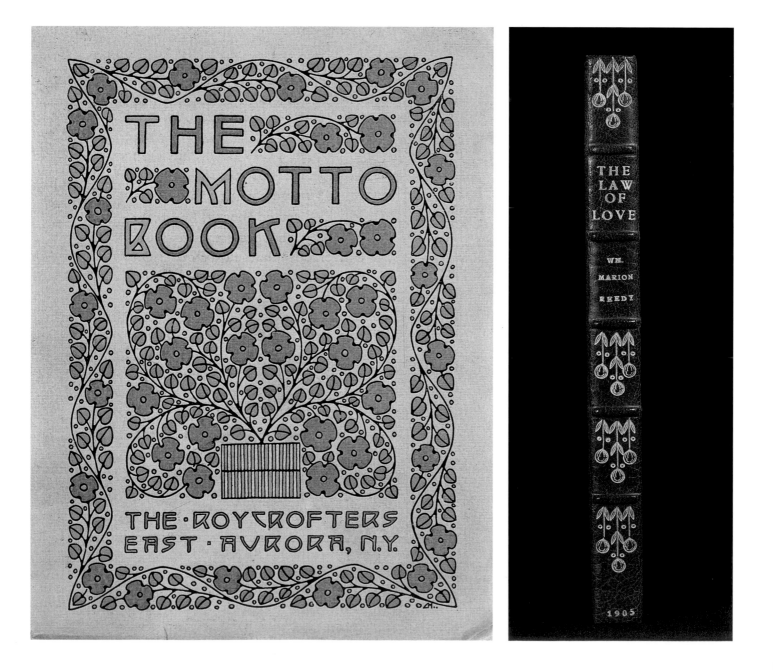

former bears the inscription *Produce great people – the rest follows.* The cabinetmaker of the two doors was probably Herbert Buffum, who joined the furniture shop at Roycroft in 1899, and they were probably carved by Tom Standeven, a woodworker who did a lot of the chair detailing at Roycroft.[4] The inscription was carefully chosen to convey the Roycroft philosophy to the visitor. Its message was drawn directly from the teachings of Morris and Ruskin and represented precisely, to the uninitiated, the values behind the Arts and Crafts Movement.

Arthur Mathews

Youth, painted by Arthur Mathews around 1917 (126), incorporates several of the major characteristics of Mathews's style. First, women are chosen in preference to men to personify youthfulness. Their robes and musical instruments are drawn from Greek antiquity, a common device used by Mathews to impart a sense of European traditionalism and continuity to his work. The painting's subdued mood is obtained by soft color tones and flat dimensional forms. Also typical of Mathews's style is the selection of the California landscape as a background. Mathews loved to paint the local coastline, particularly in the diffused light of the late afternoon. Harvey L. Jones in his monogram on Mathews and his wife provides an eloquent summary of the painting's importance:

Youth is perhaps the keystone of the Mathews *œuvre*. This work encompasses all of the individual elements of his mature style: a muralist's flat decorative approach, compositional devices inspired by Japanese prints, subdued color tonality and his organically conceived rhythms of line and pattern. Thematically it is consistent for its presentation of allegories of art and nature in California. Here the nine dancing women in the foreground suggest the muses from classical mythology while they portray the spirit of youth with their frolic in music and Dance.... The strongest thematic element of the painting is revealed in the characteristic regional landscape which completes Mathews's visual paean to youth and the arts in California.[5]

The painting's frame represents the philosophy which bound Mathews to the Arts and Crafts Movement: the elimination of the traditional distinction of fine and applied arts in the pursuit of an integrated esthetic. Predictably, the frame's classical shape, range of colors, and style of decoration complement the painting, a device used effectively by Mathews on numerous occasions.

A prolific artist, Mathews received numerous awards. In 1940, he and his wife Lucia participated in an exhibit entitled "California Art in Retrospect: 1850–1915" at the Golden Gate International Exposition.

George Grant Elmslie

A carpet designed by George Grant Elmslie in 1907 (127), while he was still a member of Louis Sullivan's staff, provides an elegant example of his attempt to achieve harmony and rhythm by the use of ornamental motifs which recurred within an interior in its furniture, rugs, windows, light fixtures, and architectural elements. It was made for the Henry B. Babson house, designed by Adler & Sullivan in Riverside, Illinois.

127   Carpet, designed by George Grant
Elmslie of Alder & Sullivan, for the Henry B.
Babson house, Riverside, Illinois (1907).
Wool, hand-knotted. Rectangular, decorated
with a pair of facing Arts and Crafts organic
motifs in pale green on a rust ground within
green, beige, rust, and brown borders. 96½in.
(245cm.) long; 44½in. (113cm.) wide.
Collection of Marilyn and Wilbert
Hasbrouck

The carpet is decorated with a pair of facing Arts and Crafts organic motifs. Use of such motifs Elmslie explained as follows:

These motifs are designed as an organic part of the structure, an efflorescence of the idea represented in the building itself.... The ornaments themselves represent the expansion of a single germinal idea and may be severe, restrained, simple or as elaborately evolved as desired for place and circumstance. After the motif is established the development of it is an orderly procession from start to finish, it is all intensely organic, proceeding from main motif to minor motifs, interrelating and to the last terminal, all of a piece....[6]

This belief was contrary to that of most of the Prairie School architects, who considered ornament superfluous.

Greene and Greene

In 1913 the architect Ralph Adams Cram wrote of the Greenes' homes,

One must see the real and revolutionary thing in its native haunts of Berkeley and Pasadena to appreciate it in all its varied charm and its striking beauty. Where it comes from heaven alone knows, but we are glad it arrived, for it gives a new zest to life, a new object for admiration. There are things in it Japanese; things that are Scandinavian; things that hint of Sikkim, Bhutan, and the fastness of Tibet, and yet it all hangs together, it is beautiful, it is contemporary, and for some reason or other it seems to fit California.... It is a wooden style built woodenly, and it has the force and integrity of Japanese architecture. Added to this is the elusive element of charm that comes only from the personality of the creator, and charm in a degree hardly matched in other modern work.[7]

The Gamble house (128, 129) completed 1908, was one of the Greenes' greatest achievements. Coming at the height of their most creative period, it is an astonishing and exciting monument to the Arts and Crafts Movement.

Within ten years of their arrival in California, the Greenes had reached a point where they could choose from among wealthy potential clients without compromising their convictions or artistic visions. At this time, David Berry Gamble, a second-generation member of the Cincinnati Gambles of Proctor & Gamble, made their acquaintance. Gamble had retired from the family firm in 1895 before moving to the West, and he was drawn to the Greenes' architecture in Pasadena, where he and his wife Mary settled.

The Gamble house was born of a single meeting with the Greene brothers. A secluded site was chosen on the outskirts of the town, one which provided a magnificent view of the San Gabriel mountains and the Arroyo Seco (now the location of the Rosebowl).

During the planning stage, Charles Greene collaborated at length with Mrs. Gamble, though the architects had been given full independence in the house's design. Four conditions were considered: climate, environment, available materials, and the owner's lifestyle. Charles Greene noted, "The intelligence of the owner as well as the ability of the architect and skill of the contractor limit the perfection of the result."[8] The *Pasadena Daily News* carried the following description of the house on 5 March 1908,

The house contained twelve rooms and the best of all available resources were used. Mahogany in the dining room, teakwood in the living room and hall, oak in the den,

128   *The David B. Gamble house, Pasadena,*
California, designed by Greene and Greene
(completed 1908).
Photo Tim Street-Porter

129   The David B. Gamble house, Pasadena,
California, designed by Greene and Greene.
Interior view with fireplace.
Photo Tim Street-Porter

and white cedar in the remainder of the house. There were five bathrooms, three luxurious sleeping porches, two enormous terraces and a garden. On the third floor is an immense billiard room that is surrounded by windows on four sides. A large kitchen, butler's pantry and screen porch along with all the supplementary closets and cupboards known to modern convenience will be on the main floor. A large bedroom with private bath is also located on the first floor, and there will be entrances on all of the terraces. On the second floor are to be five bedrooms all of large size with many windows.... The house will require a year in which to be built.

David Gamble died in 1923. The house was occupied by various members of the Gamble family until 1966, when James N. Gamble presented the deed to the house to the Board of Directors of the City of Pasadena in a joint agreement with the University of Southern California.

Frank Lloyd Wright

Plagued by personal difficulties and looking for new professional challenges, Frank Lloyd Wright headed West in the early 1920s, leaving the conservative Midwest for a freer California lifestyle. He wanted, especially, to develop a new system of building construction, one that would move him away from the horizontal Prairie School style that had become his trademark, but which he felt had begun to confine him.

Wright began to experiment with various building materials, in particular concrete, which was considered by many of his contemporaries to be cheap and ugly, a factor which probably spurred Wright's experimentation. He developed a precast concrete block method of construction, which he termed "textile block" (the blocks were reinforced with a weave of steel tie rods). Each block was hollow, its surface either plain or molded with one of the architect's characteristic geometric patterns. The interspersing of patterned and plain provided a wide range of possible decorative effects for both exteriors and interiors. In addition, some blocks were perforated, to allow the passage of air and light. The blocks' hollow core insulated the house and prevented moisture from seeping through. Intended for easy and inexpensive construction, the casting process in practice required skilled labor and, in the case of the Storer house, nearly doubled the projected budget from $15,000 to $27,000.

The house designed for Dr. John Storer of Los Angeles (130, 131), was the second of the four concrete block structures that Wright built in the early 1920s.[9] Storer had purchased a plot of land in an undeveloped, rustic area on a hill above Hollywood Boulevard. The steep elevation meant that Wright had to assemble the blocks in a series of small terraces that rise up the hillside and serve as the base for the main structure. The house comprised a series of setbacks, the terraces forming a dramatic silhouette against the hill. Wright thus made the transition from his earlier horizontal style to one with a strong vertical emphasis, achieved by the central row of four double-story piers. These, in turn, are balanced by the horizontal line of the cornice, which provides an effective counterpoint to their height. The structure is strongly Japanese, the result, no doubt, of Wright's trips between 1916 and 1922 to Tokyo to construct the Imperial Hotel.

130 *The John Storer house, 8161 Hollywood Boulevard, Los Angeles, California, designed by Frank Lloyd Wright (early 1920s). Present owner Joel Silver. Photo Richard Bryant. Architectural Photography and Picture Library*

131 The John Storer house, 8161 Hollywood Boulevard, Los Angeles, California, designed by Frank Lloyd Wright.
Interior view.
Present owner Joel Silver. Photo Richard Bryant. Architectural Photography and Picture Library

Three different geometric patterns – one perforated – are incorporated in the house's concrete block construction. The overall decorative effect is Mayan, though it is understated here in comparison to the ornamentation on Wright's nearby Hollyhock house.

The interior shows Wright's mastery of space. The house is entered through a glass door set within the window spaces between piers. The rooms on this level have Wright's characteristic low ceilings. The entry is anchored by a fireplace which has a dining area to its right. To its left a staircase descends a half-level to a small library and bedroom, while another ascends a half-level to two further bedrooms. This stair continues up and around the fireplace, leading the visitor into the main living space, a tall and imposing room which sits directly over the entry room, affording majestic panoramas of the Los Angeles valley. The fireplace is the house's focal point, around which rooms spiral off in different directions and at different angles. The result is a highly compact, and typically Wrightian interior which merges continually with the exterior, both through the windows and two patios. Dr. Storer sold the house in 1927, following which there have been four further owners. Most recently, it was purchased in 1984 by Joel Silver, a Hollywood film producer. Mr. Silver is restoring the house to its original condition, with the expertise of a team of architectural advisors and restorers, which includes the architect's grandson, Eric Lloyd Wright.[10] As Wright did not design any furniture for the house beyond a selection of bronze and glass light fixtures, Mr. Silver has furnished it with a mixture of pieces from Wright's other houses, reproductions, and works by other Arts and Crafts craftsmen.

Endnotes

Introduction

1   Stickley explained his motto in the first issue of *The Craftsman*, referring to its original use by the Flemish painter Jan Van Eyck. *Als ik kan* translates as "the best I can."

2   *The Craftsman* (October 1901): i.

3   In the early colonial period, oak was riven, or quartered along its medullary rays, rather than sawn. Sawyers could rive or split the wood much faster than they could saw it. The resulting boards were slightly wedged-shaped, and distinguished by their unique, ribboned grain structure. Stickley's wood was cut in a sawmill, but along the same quartered configuration.
     In joined construction, case pieces "hang" on a vertical structure of four stiles, to which horizontal framing members are tenoned. The "walls" of the piece are created by panels inset into grooves in the vertical and horizontal framing members. This type of construction became obsolescent in the early eighteenth century with the introduction of the dovetail joint.

4   *Repoussé* is a metalworking process in which the metal is pushed or moved into the desired design. No metal is removed in the process.

5   Hubbard adopted the Roycroft mark from the works of a medieval bookbinding monk, Cassiodorus. The orb and cross represented unity and infinity; Hubbard divided the orb into three parts signifying faith, hope and love. *See* Nancy Hubbard, ed., *Roycroft Handmade Furniture*, East Aurora, N.Y., 1973, p.58.

6   The Wiener Werkstätte was founded in Vienna in 1903 for designers and craftsmen to produce decorative arts objects. Its most influential leaders were Josef Hoffmann and Koloman Moser.

7   An exception was Parke Edwards guild, which produced glass for the Swedenborgian Church at Bryn Athyn, Pennsylvania. *See* Robert Edwards, "The Art of Work," in Wendy Kaplan, *"The Art that is Life": The Arts and Crafts Movement in America, 1875–1920*, Boston, Mass., 1987, pp.225–27

8   For more information on the numerous societies and communities of the movement throughout America, *see* Kaplan (note 7).

9   Robert Judson Clark, ed., *The Arts and Crafts Movement in America, 1876–1916*, Princeton, N.J., 1972, p.28.

10 Sharon Darling, *Chicago Furniture: Art, Craft, & Industry 1833–1916*, New York, 1984, p.250.

11 For more information on Rockledge, *see* Kaplan (note 7), pp.396–400.

12 Darling (note 10), p.257.

13 Sharon Darling, *Chicago Metalsmiths*, Chicago, Ill., 1977, p.37.

14 As quoted in Randell L. Makinson, *Greene and Greene: Furniture and Related Designs*, Santa Barbara, Calif., 1979, p.150.

15 In reduction firing the kiln is deprived of oxygen, so the fire draws oxygen from the glazes and bodies of the ceramics, thereby altering the colors.

16 For a reproduction of the brochure, *see* Neville Thompson, "Addison B. Le Boutillier: Developer of Grueby Tiles," *Tiller 2* (Nov.-Dec. 1982): 25.

17 Slip is clay in a semiliquified state, used to decorate ceramic bodies.

18 As quoted in Jessie Poesch, *Newcomb Pottery: An Enterprise for Southern Women, 1895–1940*, Exton, Pa., 1984, p.18.

19 Charles Fergus Binns (1857–1934) moved to the U.S.A. after a career at The Worcester Royal Porcelain Works in England. As the founding director of the New York School of Clayworking and Ceramics at Alfred University, Binns taught many noted potters of the American Arts and Crafts Movement.

20 Taxile Doat (1852–1939) was a famous ceramist with a personal studio at the national porcelain manufactory at

Sèvres, where he was employed. The recipient of several gold medals at international expositions, and honors from the French government, he was wooed to the United States by Edward Lewis for the University City program.

21 Frederick Hurten Rhead (1880–1942) was another successful British ceramist whose expertise was influential at various American art potteries after he immigrated in 1902. *See* Sharon Dale, *Frederick Hurten Rhead: An English Potter in America*, Erie, Pa., 1986.

Furniture

1 Margaret Edgewood, "Some Sensible Furniture," *House Beautiful* (October 1900): 655.

2 John Crosby Freeman, *The Forgotten Rebel: Gustav Stickley and His Craftsman Mission Furniture*, Watkins Glen, N.Y., 1966, p.53.

3 David M. Cathers, *Furniture of the American Arts and Crafts Movement*, New York, 1981, p.224.

4 Gustav Stickley, *The Craftsman* (January 1904): 394–96.

5 Claude Bragdon, "Harvey Ellis: A Portrait Sketch," *Architectural Review* (December 1908): 173–83.

6 *The Craftsman* (January 1904): 394–96.

7 Quoted in *Catalogue of Craftsman Furniture*, firm's booklet, 1909, p.8.

8 David M. Cathers, *Stickley Craftsman Furniture Catalogs*, New York, 1979, p.97.

9 For a comprehensive discussion of Stickley's spindle furniture, *see* Cathers (note 3), pp.147–48.

10 Charlotte Moffitt, "The Rohlfs Furniture," *House Beautiful* (December 1899): 83.

11 In "The Rohlfs Furniture," *House Beautiful* (December 1899): 83, Charlotte Moffitt described the spirit of creativity experienced on a visit to Rohlfs's makeshift attic studio where it all began:

> It is an immense room in which one finds one's self, and every foot of it used to best advantage. There are lumber, benches, lathes, tools of all kinds, paints, drawings, photographs, and furniture at every stage

of development from the first vague conception, perhaps, if one could look into Mr. Rohlfs's mind to the finished product. And here lies the difference between this shop, or one of its kind, and that of the artisan. There is that inexplicable, intangible, something in the atmosphere of the place that proclaims the presence of the creative spirit. One feels that here can be no drudgery, no *ennui*; that the endless and delightful possibilities of all this raw material are ever revealing themselves, and that the most painstaking application in working them out is Mr. Rohlfs's chiefest pleasure.

Other views of Rohlfs's house, showing a wide range of his furniture, were illustrated in *The Times*, Buffalo, New York, 2 April 1922.

12 Charles Rohlfs, "The Grain of Wood," *House Beautiful* (February 1901): 148.

13 *See* Wendy Kaplan, *"The Art that is Life": The Arts and Crafts Movement in America, 1875–1920*, Boston, Mass., 1987, p.95, fig.35.

14 Frank Lloyd Wright, "The Art and Craft of the Machine," in *Catalogue of the Fourteenth Annual Exhibition of the Chicago Architectural Club* (Chicago Architectural Club), 1901, no pagination.

15 From the Ashbee Journals, December 1900 (ms. in Cambridge University Library).

16 Frank Lloyd Wright, *A Testament*, New York, 1957, p.205.

17 For a wall lamp of similar design also from the Wayzata house, *see* Edgar Kaufmann, Jr., *Frank Lloyd Wright at the Metropolitan Museum of Art*, museum booklet, 1982, p.30.

18 David A. Hanks, *The Decorative Designs of Frank Lloyd Wright*, New York, 1979, p.113.

19 Quoted in *The Arts and Crafts Movement in America*, exhibition catalogue, The Art Museum, Princeton, 1972, p.45.

20 Dard Hunter's son verified in a telephone conversation, 12 September 1986, that the bookcase was by his father, but pointed out that there is no existing record confirming that it was made while Hunter was at Roycroft (1904–10).

21 Dard Hunter II, *The Life Work of Dard Hunter*, Chillicothe, N.Y., 1981, vol.I, p.118.

22 For biographical information on Elmslie, *see* Brian A. Spencer, *The Prairie School Tradition*, New York, 1979, p.120.

23 For a concise biography of Purcell, *see* David Gebhard, "Purcell and Elmslie, Architects," *Prairie School Review* (July 1965): 5–13.

24 Quoted in Marian Page, *Furniture Designed by Architects*, London, 1980, p.114.

25 For a comprehensive biography of Maher, *see* J. William Rudd, "George W. Maher: Architect of the Prairie School," *The Prairie School Review* 1 (1964): 5–10.

26 Page (note 24), p.118.

27 For biographical information on the Mathews, *see* Harvey L. Jones, *Mathews Masterpieces of the California Decorative Style*, New York, 1985.

28 No contemporary photographs of Mathews interiors are believed to exist.

29 *See* Jones (note 27), p.86.

30 *Ibid.*, pp.89, 91.

Ceramics

1 Mrs. Nichols did not participate in the 1876 Philadelphia Exposition but she viewed the exhibits of the early promoter of women potters in Cincinnati, Mary Louise McLaughlin. For a biography of McLaughlin, *see* Paul Evans, *Art Pottery of the United States*, New York, 1974, pp.145–50.

2 Marshall Fry, Jr., "Notes from the Paris Exposition," *Keramic Studio* (September 1900): 99.

3 Quoted in Kenneth R. Trapp, *Ode to Nature: Flowers and Landscapes of the Rookwood Pottery 1880–1940*, Santa Barbara, Calif., 1980, p.30.

4 Herbert Peck, *The Book of Rookwood Pottery*, New York, 1968, p.145.

5 *Cincinnati Enquirer*, 25 August 1945, p.56; quoted in Kenneth R. Trapp, *Towards the Modern Style: Rookwood Pottery The Later Years: 1915–1950,*

exhibition catalogue, the Jordan-Volpe Gallery, New York, 1983, p.32.

6 For biographical information on Van Briggle, *see Van Briggle Pottery: The Early Years*, exhibition catalogue, Colorado Springs Fine Arts Center, 1975; and Dorothy McGraw Bogue, *The Van Briggle Story*, Colorado Springs, 1968. Further biographical sources are given in Eugene Hecht, "Artus Van Briggle: The Formative Years," *Arts and Crafts Quarterly* (January 1987): 12.

7 For discussion of the "Lorelei" vase and the date it was made, *see* Hecht (note 6): 10.

8 George D. Galloway, "The Van Briggle Pottery," *Brush and Pencil* (October 1901): 5.

9 The "Despondency" model has been illustrated widely; *see*, for example, *House and Garden* (October 1903): 166, 167; and *Pottery and Glass* (August 1908): 3.

10 Galloway (note 8): 7, 8.

11 Irene Sargent, "Chinese Pots and Modern Faience," *The Craftsman* (June 1903): 418, 419.

12 Galloway (note 8).

13 For a comprehensive biography of Nicholson, *see* Jessie Poesch, *Newcomb Pottery*, exhibition catalogue, Exton, Pa., 1984, p.103.

14 For a biography of Meyer, *see* Poesch (note 13), p.94.

15 Sheerer, "Joseph Meyer, Potter – A Picturesque Figure," *The Newcomb Arcade* (June 1910): 16.

16 Lota Lee Troy, "Newcomb Pottery Changes Designs of 35 Years Standing," *Item* (2 March 1932).

17 For a biography of Simpson, *see* Poesch (note 13), p.105.

18 For an example of this motif, *see* Poesch (note 13), p.139.

19 *See Brush and Pencil* (January 1902): 241.

20 *See* Mary Chase Perry, "Grueby Potteries," *Keramic Studio* (April 1901): 251; and *Brush and Pencil* (January 1902): 241.

21 Martin Eidelberg, "The Ceramic Art of William H. Grueby," *The American Connoisseur* (September 1973): 49. Eidelberg's article gives a summary of information on Grueby and Delaherche given by Perry (note 20).

22 *The Studio, XII* (1898): 144, 116; *see also* Eidelberg.

23 Eidelberg (note 21).

24 One example of this model, included in the Grueby exhibition at the Everson Museum of Art, Syracuse, N.Y., in 1981 (exhibition catalogue, p.4., fig.2, cat.10), is now in the collection of the Cooper Hewitt Museum, New York. Another is in the collection of the Museum of Modern Art, New York. The fourth, modeled by Ellen R. Farrington, is in a private collection.

25 For examples of these early tiles and plaques, *see* Eidelberg (note 21): 50–51.

26 The Owens Pottery Company copied Grueby's *cloisonné* technique in a range of later plaques depicting landscapes and farmyard animals.

27 *International Studio* (Nov. 1904–Feb. 1905): XCI–XCVII. Another oxen fireplace surround, identical except that the image is reversed and the four lower side tiles are absent, is in the collection of Mr. R. A. Ellison.

28 *Keramic Studio* (February 1905): 216.

29 *The Craftsman* (December 1914): 297.

30 *See The Brickbuilder, XV* (1906): 107; and *Grueby*, exhibition catalogue, the Everson Museum of Art, Syracuse, N.Y., 1981, pp.14–15.

31 An article in *Pottery and Glass*, (April 1911): 17, provided different terminology for two of the five hues: "apple blossom" and "matte" for "deep rose" and "old rose."

32 *Pottery and Glass* (August 1910): 16.

33 The second piece given to the Newark Museum, with a "rose matte" glaze, is illustrated in Ulysses G. Dietz, *The Newark Museum Collection of American Art Pottery*, the Newark Museum, Newark, N.J., 1984, p.53. A third "Famille Rose" vase in the Museum's collection, purchased in 1915, is illustrated on p.60.

34 *Pottery and Glass* (August 1910): 16.

35 Charles F. Binns, "In Defense of Fire," *The Craftsman* (March 1903): 369–72.

36 "Jersey Pottery Wins Honors at International Fair," *Pottery and Glass* (July 1915): 9–10.

37 *See Keramic Studio* (August 1901): 82–83.

38 The model is also referred to as a "fern tendril," *see*, for example, Hugh F. McKean, *The "Lost" Treasures of Louis Comfort Tiffany*, New York, 1980, p.207.

39 For a comprehensive discussion of Tiffany pottery and illustrations of examples decorated with plants and cereals, *see* Martin Eidelberg, "Tiffany Favrile Pottery," *The Connoisseur* (September 1968): 57–61.

40 Three fish bowls in the collection of the Morse Gallery in Winterpark, Florida, illustrate how different in feeling are the effects imparted by three different finishes to the same model (*see* McKean, note 38, p.214). One is in a bisque glaze, another in bronze, and the third in a pale green. This helps to conceal the fact that the pieces are duplicates. Further variation occurs in identical pieces applied with the same colored glaze: the free flow of the glaze into the recessed parts of a relief design, and the uncontrollable, sometimes accidental, effects of the kiln, generate subtle discrepancies and individuality. Most applications were monochromatic, the glaze often accented with random splotching or crystalline inclusions. A glossy olive-black, caused by excess glaze gathering in the edges of the design, traces the primary images, adding strong emphasis.

41 One of the first references to Teco ware appears to be that of Walter Ellsworth Gray, who wrote in February 1902 in *Brush and Pencil*, p.289, that "this beautiful product has as yet scarcely been introduced to the public." A later reference by Charles Crosby – *Arts and Decoration* (March 1911): 214 – states that Teco was distributed nationwide in 1904, suggesting that it took Gates two years to set up sales outlets and to build up his inventory.

42 For a biography of Gates, *see* Ralph and Terry Kovel, *The Kovels' Collector's Guide to American Art Pottery*, New York, 1974, p.262.

43 Crosby (note 41).

44 *See Brush and Pencil* (April 1905): 74. Though some pieces were in fact thrown, contemporary literature implies that these were either experimental or special orders.

45 Kovel (note 42), p.264.

46 Gates's preference for his mat green glazes is noted by Evelyn Marie Stuart, "Teco Pottery and Faience Tile," *Fine Arts Journal* (June 1909): 103; and by Walter Ellsworth Gray, "Latter-Day Developments in

American Pottery – II," *Brush and Pencil* (February 1902): 292.

47 William Harold Edgar, "The Teco Pottery," *International Studio* (January 1909) supplement: XXIX.

48 For a short biography of Albert, *see* Susan Stuart Frackleton, "Our American Potteries," *The Sketch Book* (October 1905): 78.

49 Examples of floral vases by these designers are illustrated in *Teco*, firm's catalogue (c. 1905), unpaginated.

50 Susan Stuart Frackleton, "Our American Potteries: Teco Ware," *The Sketch Book* (September 1905): 18.

51 Jonathan A. Rawson, Jr., "Teco and Robineau Pottery," *House Beautiful* (April 1913): 151.

52 For biographies of Weller, *see*, for example, Lucile Henzke, *American Art Pottery*, Nashville, Tenn., 1970, pp.33–121; and Paul Evans, *Art Pottery of the United States*, New York, 1974, pp.323–29.

53 For a contemporary discussion of Sicard's work at Weller, *see* Mary Elizabeth Cook, "Our American Potteries – Weller Ware," *The Sketch Book* (May 1906): 345–46.

54 For a biography of Brouwer, *see* W.P. Jervis, *The Encyclopedia of Ceramics*, New York, 1902, pp.72, 74.

55 Quoted in Frederick H. Rhead, "Theophilus A. Brouwer, Jr., Maker of Iridescent Glazed Faience," *The Potter* (January 1917): 48. For a contemporary article on Brouwer, see Anne Winslow Crane, "The Middle Lane Pottery," *The Art Intercharge* (August 1900): 32, 33; *see also* Paul Evans, *Art Pottery of the United States*, New York, 1974, pp.173–76.

56 *House Beautiful* (September 1897): 91, 92.

57 For a comprehensive history of Robertson and the Dedham Pottery, *see* Lloyd E. Hawes, *The Dedham Pottery and the Earlier Robertson's Chelsea Potteries*, Dedham Historical Society, Dedham, Mass., 1968.

58 Paul Evans's book, *Art Pottery of the United States*, New York, 1974, remains the most complete reference on Brauckman. *See also* Hazel V. Bray, *The Potter's Art in California 1885 to 1955*, The Oakland Museum Art Department, Oakland, Calif., 1980, p.17; and *Californian Design 1910*, Santa Barbara, Calif., 1980, pp.68–69, 76.

59 Evans, pp. 116–17.

60 *Grand Feu Ceramics: A Practical Treatise on the Making of Fine Porcelain and Grès Flammés*, with an introductory essay by Professor Charles F. Binns, Syracuse, N.Y., 1905.

61 For a typical discussion of Doat's work in France, *see* W. P. Jervis, "Taxile Doat," *Keramic Studio* (July 1902): 54–55; and Irene Sargent, "Taxile Doat," *Keramic Studio* (December 1906): 171–73, 193.

62 The first model was illustrated in *The Sketch Book* (January 1906): 232. Either the illustration shown has been reversed, or the design on the first vase ran in the opposite direction. This second model is undated but its year of creation was listed as 1908 in *High Fire Porcelains: Adelaide Alsop Robineau Potter*, exhibition booklet, the Panama–Pacific Exposition, San Francisco, 1915, entry no.2, listed at $75; it was described as "the last of two vases made with this decoration" when illustrated in *Glass and Pottery* (March 1909): 11.

63 *Dekorative Vorbilder* 12 (1901), pl. 55; illustrated in Peg Weiss, ed., *Adelaide Alsop Robineau*, Syracuse, N.Y., 1981, p.82, ill.98.

64 F. H. Rhead, *The Potter* (February 1917): 87; quoted in Peg Weiss, ed., *Adelaide Alsop Robineau*, Syracuse, N.Y., 1981, p.215, ftnote 18.

65 Excising consists of the creation of a relief decoration on porcelain by scraping away the background until the design stands out. The reverse of incised decoration, by which the design is carved into the surface of the body, excising is an alternative, but more painstaking, technique to *pâte-sur-pâte*.

66 F. H. Rhead, *The Potter* (February 1917): 87; quoted in Peg Weiss, ed., *Adelaide Alsop Robineau*, Syracuse, N.Y., 1981, p.215, ftnote 18.

67 Samuel Robineau, "The Robineau Porcelains," *Keramic Studio* (August 1911): 84. Another summary of the vase's theme by Samuel Robineau is given in *Pottery and Glass* (February 1911): 19.

68 Samuel Robineau recalled the event in *Design* (April 1929): 205–206.

69 *High Fire Porcelains Adelaide Alsop Robineau Potter*, exhibition booklet, the Panama–Pacific Exposition, San Francisco, 1915, unpaginated.

70 For a comprehensive summary of the influences on

Robineau's style, *see* Martin Eidelberg in Peg Weiss, ed., *Adelaide Alsop Robineau*, Syracuse, N.Y., 1981, chap. 2.

71 Paul Evans, *Art Pottery of the United States*, New York, 1974, p.236.

72 For a biography of Rhead, *see* Timothy J. Anderson, Eudorah M. Moore, and Robert W. Winter, *California Design 1910*, Santa Barbara, Calif., 1974, pp.72, 76.

73 Robert W. Blasberg, *George E. Ohr and His Biloxi Art Pottery*, Port Jervis, N.Y., 1973, p.10.

74 *Ceramic Art* (April 1953): 140; quoted in *Art Pottery of the United States, An Encyclopedia of Producers and their Marks*, New York, 1974, p.30.

75 One of Ohr's molds for the spout is illustrated in Robert W. Blasberg, *The Unknown Ohr*, Milford, Pa., 1986, p.28, fig.14.

76 Edwin Atlee Barber, *Marks of American Potters*, Philadelphia, Pa., 1904.

77 At this time, they were bought by a dealer, J. W. Carpenter.

78 For a history of Marblehead Pottery, *see* Gail Pike Hercher, "Marblehead Pottery," *Marblehead Magazine* (April 1980): 21–23.

79 A complete history of the Overbeck family and pottery is provided by Kathleen R. Postle in *The Chronicle of the Overbeck Pottery*, Indiana Historical Society, Indianapolis, Ind., 1978.

80 Postle, p.55.

81 *Ibid.*

Metal and Silver

1 According to information from the Jordan-Volpe Gallery, New York, Elizabeth Eleanor D'Arcy Gaw was born in Montreal and graduated from the School of the Art Institute of Chicago. In 1901 she cofounded a group called "The Crafters" with the architect Lawrence Buck and the decorator Mary Mower. In 1904 she moved to the West Coast, where she was soon back in San Jose. She appears in the town's directory as a designer until 1919.

2 *The Philistine* (June 1899): 1.

3 For brief biographies of Denslow and Karl Kipp, *see* Charles F. Hamilton, *Roycroft Collectibles*, p.75.

4 For an illustration of the Roycroft seahorse logo, *see* Hamilton, pp.29, 33.

5 A vase with both Roycroft and Kipp marks was included in the 1972 Princeton show; *see* Robert Judson Clark, ed., *The Arts and Crafts Movement in America 1876–1916*, Princeton, N.J., 1972, p.50, no.59.

6 Typical Kipp and Jennings designs for Roycroft cigarette boxes and humidors are illustrated in *The Book of the Roycrofters*, firm's catalogue, 1919, pp.18, 73.

7 Quoted in David A. Hanks, *The Decorative Designs of Frank Lloyd Wright*, New York, 1979, pp.69–70.

8 Two examples of this model were included in a Wright grouping illustrated on the cover of the catalogue of the Chicago Architectural Club exhibition which opened at the Art Institute of Chicago in the spring of 1902. *See Frank Lloyd Wright and Viollet-le-Duc Organic Architecture and Design from 1850 to 1950*, exhibition catalogue, the Armstrong Gallery, New York, 12 March – 5 April 1986, p.4.

9 It is not known whether Wright commissioned Miller to custom-produce these pieces for the house in which they were to be used, or whether he made them for stock, which would then be available for future commissions.

10 Although contemporary documentation describes the T-shaped plaque as copperplated, examination today indicates rather that it is a bronze alloy with a high copper content.

11 For a discussion of Sullivan's evolving style of decoration, *see Louis H. Sullivan Architectural Ornament Collection*, Edwardsville, Ill., 1981.

12 *Ibid.*, pp. 17–18.

13 The original working drawing for the piece is in the collection of the Tiffany & Company archives.

14 For detailed discussion of L. C. Tiffany's enamelware, *see* Robert Koch, *Louis C. Tiffany's Glass-Bronzes-*

Lamps, pp.148, 152–54; and Hugh F. McKean, *The "Lost" Treasures of Louis Comfort Tiffany*, pp.237–42.

15 *See* Koch and McKean.

16 *See* Elliot Evans, *Silver in the Golden State*, The Oakland Museum History Department, 1986, p.16*ff*, for a comprehensive history of the firm.

17 *Evans.*, p.32.

18 *Ibid.*, for a selection of flatware in these patterns.

19 Jarvie advertised his candlesticks from 1901 in *House Beautiful*, followed by *The Craftsman, Fine Arts Journal*, and *Arts and Decoration*.

20 Anon, "Work of Robert Jarvie," *The Craftsman* (December 1903): 273.

21 Sharon S. Darling, *Chicago Metalsmiths*, Chicago, Ill., pp.55–56.

22 For examples of early candlesticks by Jarvie, *see Keramic Studio* (July 1905): 66; and *The Craftsman* (December 1903): 276.

23 Roger Caye, "Paul Revere, Silversmith, and Modern Emulators," *Arts and Decoration* (August 1914): 386.

24 Files of the Chicago Historical Society, quoted in Robert Judson Clark, *The Arts and Crafts Movement in America 1876–1916*, Princeton, N.J., 1972, p.76.

25 Caye (*see* note 23); Jarvie obtained a plaster cast of a prehistoric Indian (cliff dweller) motif from a bowl in the Field Museum of Natural History, which he adapted for his design for the presentation punch bowl. The bowl is illustrated in Clark (note 24) p.75, no.97.

26 For a comprehensive biography of Welles and the Kalo shops, *see* Darling (note 21), pp.45–55.

27 For a concise discussion of the different Kalo hallmarks, *see* Walter Scott Braznell's catalogue entry in Wendy Kaplan, *"The Art that is Life": The Arts and Crafts Movement in America, 1875–1920*, Museum of Fine Arts, Boston, 1987, p.280, no.142.

28 For similar Ashbee designs, *see* illustrations in Mervyn Levy, *Liberty Style*, New York, 1986; and Victor Arwas, *Liberty Style*, 1983.

29 For further discussion, *see* Braznell (note 27), pp.279–80, no.141.

30 For a history of the Hull-House Shops, *see* Darling (note 21), p.36.

31 For a biographical sketch on Mrs. Glessner, *see* Darling (note 21), pp.67, 68.

32 For a comprehensive biography of Lebolt, *see* Darling (note 21), pp.105–10.

Lighting and Windows

1 The residences that Wright was commissioned to build for Bradley, and his brother-in-law, Warren Hickox, in Kankakee, Illinois, marked the beginning of Wright's Prairie Style period. He was introduced to Bradley and Hickox by Charles E. Roberts, founder and President of the American Steel Screw Company, who had commissioned him to remodel the interior of his Oak Park home. Roberts was an admirer of Wrights, and a neighbor of Bradley and Hickox. His wife and Bradley's wife were sisters and Hickox was their brother.

2 *See* David A. Hanks, *The Decorative Designs of Frank Lloyd Wright*, New York, 1979, pl.2.

3 The Dana house glass includes a wide range of Wright's decorative and technical innovations. Stylistically, there are abstract insect themes such as the repeating butterfly motifs on the entrance surround and the angular geometry of the barrel-vaulted skylight in the hallway which leads off it. The incorporation in the designs of multiple thin parallel lines, many only ¼ in. wide, required a precision in their execution seldom demanded of a glass craftsman. Wright also utilized different widths of zinc came in some panels to provide additional emphasis, in this manner making them an integral part of the design. The glass "curtain" in the house's ballroom includes another innovative glass technique, in this instance one that Wright did not repeat on any other occasion: nine free-hanging panels suspended from a wooden frame inside the actual glass window.

4 This influence was apparent also at the time in a remarkably similar leaded lamp shade designed by Louis Comfort Tiffany, and listed in the Tiffany Studios 1906 price list as "model #1524, 25 in. Lotus, Pagoda."

5 The Linden Glass Company was established in 1890 by Frank L. Linden as part of Spierling & Linden

Associates, a decorating firm which he had formed with Ernest Spierling in Chicago eight years earlier. The firm offered a wide range of interior furnishings, including murals, furniture and textile designs, stained glass, and mosaics. The art glass windows were made by a dozen artisans in the rear of the company's offices at 1216 Michigan Avenue, Chicago. In 1892 Ernest J. Wagner was first listed as manager of the Linden Glass Company.

6 Frank Lloyd Wright, "In the Cause of Architecture," *Architectural Record* (July 1928): 13.

7 The window is shown *in situ* in Henry-Russell Hitchcock, *In the Nature of Materials*, New York, 1975, fig.104; Wright had used a variation of this design in the Willits house in 1901, *see Frank Lloyd Wright*, exhibition catalogue, Kelmscott Gallery, Chicago, p.8, fig.3.

8 Frank Lloyd Wright, "In the Cause of Architecture: The Meaning of Materials; Stone," *The Architectural Record* (May 1928) : 350; quoted in *Frank Lloyd Wright: A Modern Aesthetic*, exhibition catalogue, Struve Gallery, Chicago, 1986, no.4.

9 Grant Carpenter Mason, *Frank Lloyd Wright to 1910*, New York, 1958, p.147.

10 Completed in 1914, the playhouse was a compact, cruciform structure with a flat slab roof. Incorporated into it were a stage, kitchen, and workshop. The school was shortlived. It began by teaching only one grade – that for Elizabeth Coonley's age group – but as she advanced additional classes were added. By 1915 Elizabeth had completed eight grades (in six years) and was ready to enter the Francis Parker School in Chicago. An offer to the Riverside Board of Education to take over the project was declined, so Mrs. Coonley closed the building. Two years later her husband was offered the position of head of public relations for the Christian Science Church in Washington, D.C. The estate was purchased by Peter Kroehler, of the Chicago-based Kroehler Furniture Co., who occupied the house from 1917 until his death in 1951. His widow sold it within a short time to a Chicago developer, Arnold Skow, who divided the complex into four sections. The main house was converted into a duplex apartment building. The playhouse, sold to someone else, was adapted into a family home. Further remodeling of the playhouse followed over the years, and all but two of the windows have been removed. The present owners are restoring it to its original cruciform shape, a process requiring considerable energy and expense. Elizabeth Coonley, who married an architect, Waldron Faulkner,

in the 1930s, visited the property a few times prior to her death in 1985.

11 No record appears to have survived of the names or model numbers assigned by Grueby to his wares. This is substantiated by the fact that most pieces bear no identification beyond an impressed firm's mark. The number *17* on this base is therefore rare, and indicates that the model was introduced shortly after the firm was incorporated in 1897. The leaf pattern on the base, which protrudes well beyond that on most models, is likewise unrecorded, suggesting that it may have been a unique commission.

12 The mustard glaze on this base varied in hue from its introduction, *c.* 1898, to that of later years, providing a key with which to date a piece. The yellowish tone of this example was replaced towards 1910 with a darker, pumpkin-brown color.

13 The color postcard, printed in Germany, bears the trademark *Newvochrome*. It was one of several postcards of the Roycroft buildings sold on the Roycroft campus at the time.

14 Dard Hunter II, *The Life Work of Dard Hunter*, Chillicothe, New York, 1981, vol. I, p.167.

15 *See* Nancy Hubbard, ed., *Roycroft Handmade Furniture*, East Aurora, New York, 1973, p.11.

16 *See*, for example, model no.0126, *Roycroft Furniture*, firm's catalogue, East Aurora, New York, 1906, p.17.

17 *See* Dard Hunter II (note 14).

18 Hunter's provisional sketch for the panel of the printer included the accompanying inscription, *The Printer*, in the upper scrolled entablature. The lettering was omitted from the finished glass panel, as were the matching ones for the architect and sculptor. The sketch is illustrated in Dard Hunter II (note 14), p.176.

19 Referring to contemporary German reviews such as *Deutsche Kunst und Dekoration*, he later noted, "these magazines were a monthly inspiration, and many of the commercial designs I made during my early years at the shop show this influence."

20 As quoted in Timothy J. Anderson, Eudorah M. Moore, and Robert W. Winter, *California Design 1910*, Santa Barbara, Calif., 1974, p.78.

21 *Pottery and Glass* (April 1911): 8.

Miscellaneous

1   *See* Jean-François Vilain, "The Last Ride," *III Arts and Crafts Quarterly* (October 1986): 1, 7–8.

2   *See,* for example, Mary Roelofs Stott, *Elbert Hubbard: Rebel with Reverence*, New York, 1975, p.78*ff.*

3   For a brief biography of Kinder and his bookbindings department, *see* Charles F. Hamilton, *Roycroft Collectibles*, New York, 1980, pp.88–91.

4   For a discussion of the cabinetmakers at Roycroft, *see* Hamilton (note 3).

5   Harvey L. Jones, *Mathews Masterpieces of the California Decorative Style*, New York, 1985, p.66.

6   Quoted in Marian Page, *Furniture Designed by Architects*, New York, 1983, p.115.

7   Page (note 6), p.118.

8   Charles Sumner Greene, "Bungalows," *The Western Architect* (July 1908): 3–5.

9   For a comprehensive discussion of the house, *see* Paul Goldberger, "A Lasting Wright Legacy," the *New York Times Magazine*, 16 June 1985, section 6, pp.54–57,72.

10   Several articles have been written since 1985 on the restoration undertaken by Mr. Silver. *See,* for example, Daniel Cohen, "Hollywood Discovers the Wright Stuff," *Historic Preservation* (August 1985): 20–25; Pilar Viladas, "Invisible Reweaving," *Progressive Architecture* (November 1985): 112–17: and Hunter Drohojowska, "Joel Silver's Wright Stuff," *LA Style* (July 1985): 38–44.

Acknowledgments

Alastair Duncan gratefully acknowledges:

Chicago Historical Society: Sharon Darling, Olivia Mahoney

The Art Institute of Chicago: Milo M. Naeve

The Brooklyn Museum: Dianne H. Pilgrim, Christopher Wilk

Museum of American Art of the Carnegie Institute in Pittsburgh: Philip Johnston

Cooper Hewitt Library: Margaret Lucaus, Librarian

The Frank Lloyd Wright Memorial Foundation, Taliesin West: Bruce Pfeiffer

The Newark Museum: Ulysses Dietz

The Oakland Museum: Kenneth Trapp

Architectural Drawings Collection of the University of California, Santa Barbara: David Gebhard

The Gamble House, Pasadena: Randell L. Makinson

The Cincinnati Historical Society

The Minneapolis Historical Society

The Pasadena Historical Society

David A. Hanks & Associates: David Hanks

The Metropolitan Museum of Art: Craig Miller

The Hollyhock House: Virginia Kazor, Curator

The Dana-Thomas House: Dr. Donald Hallmark, Curator

The Frank Lloyd Wright Home & Studio Foundation: Donald Kalec, Director of Research & Restoration

Frank Lloyd Wright Home Tours, Riverside, Illinois: Jan Kolar, Chairman

Department of Art History, State University of New York at Buffalo: Dr. Jack Quinan

The Storer House: Joel Silver, and Peter Purens, Restorer

David Rago

Library of the National Museum of American Art, Smithsonian Institution, Washington, D.C.: Pat Lynagh, Librarian

Cincinnati Museum of Art: Anita Ellis

Virginia Museum of Fine Arts: Frederick R. Brandt

Everson Museum of Art: Rosemarie Romano, Librarian

Jeremy Adamson

W. Scott Braznell

Martin Eidelberg

The Cleveland Museum of Art: Henry Hawley

The Roycroft Inn: Robert Rust, Kitty Turgeon

Boice Lydell

Robert A. Ellison

Gordon Gray

Amiel and Gabriela Brown

Seymour and Ruth Geringer

William and Marcia Goodman

Edgar O. Smith

Bryce R. Bannatyne, Jr., of P.G. Pugsley and Son

Eric Silver

The Morse Gallery of Art, Winter Park, Florida: David P. Donaldson

Tiffany & Co.: Janet Zapata

Tod M. Volpe and Beth Cathers gratefully acknowledge:

Marcia Anderson

Reenie Bisbee

Fredrick Brandt

Sharon Darling

Ulysses Dietz

David P. Donaldson

Christine Droll

Alice Cooney Frelinghuysen

Victoria Garvin

Hollister Gignoux

Donald P. Hallmark

Phillip Johnston

Ronald Kuchta

Sydney and Frances Lewis

David R. McFadden

Randall Mackinson

Olivia Mahoney

R. Craig Miller

Joy Morrell

Milo Naeve

Sarah C. Nichols

Alice Nightingale

Donald Peirce

Barbara Perry

John Rexine

Tamara Smith

Kenneth Trapp

Barbara A. Whalen

Lenders

Mr. and Mrs. John M. Angelo

The Art Institute of Chicago

Mr. and Mrs. Milton Brechner

Gabriela Brown
Beth L. Cathers
David and Beth Cathers
Rob Carr
Darrel Couturier
Chicago Historical Society
Cooper-Hewitt Museum
The Dana-Thomas House
Dillenberg-Espinar Collection
R. A. Ellison
The Everson Museum of Art
Fer-Duc, Inc.
Susan Fetterolf and Jeffrey Gorrin
The Gamble House
Ruth and Seymour Geringer
William and Marcia Goodman
Mr. and Mrs. Jack B. Hartog
Marilyn and Wilbert Hasbrouck
High Museum of Art
Jederman Collection, N. A.
Jordan-Volpe Gallery
The Kay Collection

Los Angeles County Museum of Art
Boice Lydell
The Manney Collection
James and Janeen Marrin
Metropolitan Museum of Art
Minnesota Historical Society Collections
The Charles Hosmer Morse Museum of American Art
Museum of Art, Carnegie Institute
The Newark Museum
Tazio Nuvolari
The Oakland Museum
Max Palevsky
P. G. Pugsley & Son Antiques
Joel Silver
Kitty Turgeon-Robert Rust
    Roycroft Inn and Shops
Tiffany and Company
Virginia Museum of Fine Arts
Tod M. Volpe
Daniel Wolf
And Ten Anonymous Lenders

Bibliography

Anderson, Timothy J.; Moore, Eudorah; and Winter, Robert W., *California Design 1910*, Santa Barbara, Calif., 1974

Anscombe, Isabella, and Gere, Charlotte, *Arts and Crafts in Britain and America*, New York, 1978

The Art of California: Selected Works from the Collection of the Oakland Museum, Oakland, Calif., 1984

Art Pottery of the United States, An Encyclopedia of Producers and Their Marks, New York, 1974

Barber, Edwin Atlee, *Marks of American Potters*, Philadelphia, Pa., 1904

Blasberg, Robert W., *George E. Ohr and His Biloxi Art Pottery*, Port Jervis, N.Y., 1973
_____*The Unknown Ohr*, Milford, Pa., 1986
_____and Bohdan, Carol L., *Fulper Art Pottery: An Aesthetic Appreciation, 1909–1929*, New York, 1979

The Book of the Roycrofters, Being a Catalog of Copper, Leather, and Books, East Aurora, N.Y., 1977

Brandt, Frederick R., *Late 19th and Early 20th Century Decorative Arts*, The Virginia Museum of Fine Arts, Richmond, Virginia, 1985

Bray, Hazel V., *The Potter's Art in California 1885 to 1955*, Oakland, Calif., 1980

Brooks, H. Allen, *Frank Lloyd Wright and the Prairie School*, New York, 1984

Cathers, David M. *Furniture of the American Arts and Crafts Movement*, New York, 1981
_____*Stickley Craftsman Furniture Catalogs*, New York, 1979

Clark, Garth, and Hughto, Margaret, *A Century of Ceramics in the United States*, New York, 1979

Clark, Robert Judson, ed., *The Arts and Crafts Movement in America 1876–1916*, Princeton, N.J., 1972

Collected Works of Gustav Stickley, New York, 1981

Craftsman Hand-Wrought Metal Work in Iron, Copper and Brass, booklet of the Craftsman Workshop, Eastwood, N.Y., n.d.

Dale, Sharon, *Frederick Hurten Rhead: An English Potter in America*, Erie, Pa., 1986

Danforth Museum of Art, *On the Threshold of Modern Design: The Arts and Crafts Movement in America*, Danforth, Mass., 1984

Darling, Sharon, *Chicago Ceramics and Glass*, Chicago, Ill., 1979
_____*Chicago Furniture: Art, Craft & Industry 1833–1983*, New York, 1984
_____*Chicago Metalsmiths*, Chicago, Ill., 1977

Davidson, Marshall B., and Stillinger, Elizabeth, *The American Wing at the Metropolitan Museum of Art*, New York, 1985

Evans, Elliot, *Silver in the Golden State*, Oakland, Calif., 1986

Evans, Paul, *Art Pottery of the United States, An Encyclopedia of Producers and Their Marks*, New York, 1974

Freeman, John Crosby, *The Forgotten Rebel: Gustav Stickley and His Craftsman Mission Furniture*, Watkins Glen, N.Y., 1966

Gray, S., and Edwards, R., eds., *Collected Works of Gustav Stickley*, New York, 1981

Hamilton, Charles F., *Roycroft Collectibles*, Cranbury, N.J., 1980

Hanks, David A., *The Decorative Designs of Frank Lloyd Wright*, New York, 1979
_____*Innovative Furniture in America*, New York, 1981

Hand-Wrought Metal Work, Eastwood, N.Y., n.d.

Hawes, Lloyd E., *The Dedham Pottery and the Earlier Robertson's Chelsea Potteries*, Dedham, Mass., 1968

Heinz, Thomas A., *Frank Lloyd Wright*, New York, 1982

Henzke, Lucile, *American Art Pottery*, Nashville, Tenn., 1970

Hitchcock, Henry-Russell, *In the Nature of Materials: The Buildings of Frank Lloyd Wright 1887–1941*, New York, 1975

Hubbard, Nancy, ed., *Roycroft Handmade Furniture*, East Aurora, N.Y., 1973

Hunter, Dard, *My Life with Paper: An Autobiography*, New York, 1958

Hunter, Dard, II, *The Life Work of Dard Hunter*, Chillicothe, N.Y., 1981

Jervis, W.P., *The Encyclopedia of Ceramics*, New York, 1902

Jones, Harvey L., *Mathews Masterpieces of the California Decorative Style*, New York, 1985

Kaplan, Wendy, *"The Art that is Life": The Arts & Crafts Movement in America, 1875–1920*, Boston, 1987

Keen, Kirsten Hoving, *American Art Pottery 1875–1930*, Wilmington, Del., 1978

Koch, Robert, *Louis C. Tiffany's Glass—Bronzes—Lamps*, New York, 1971

Kovel, Ralph and Terry, *The Kovels' Collectors' Guide to American Art Pottery*, New York, 1974

Louis H. Sullivan Architectural Ornament Collection, Edwardsville, Ill., 1981

McKean, Hugh F., *The "Lost" Treasures of Louis Comfort Tiffany*, New York, 1980

Makinson, Randell L., *Greene and Greene Architecture as a Fine Art*, Santa Barbara, Calif., 1977
————*Greene and Greene Furniture and Related Designs*, Santa Barbara, Calif., 1979

Mason, Grant Carpenter, *Frank Lloyd Wright to 1910*, New York, 1958

Naylor, Gillian, *The Arts and Crafts Movement*, London, 1971

Page, Marian, *Furniture Designed by Architects*, New York, 1983

Peck, Herbert, *The Book of Rookwood Pottery*, New York, 1968

Pevsner, Nikolaus, *Pioneers of the Modern Movement, from William Morris to Walter Gropius*, London, 1936

Poesch, Jessie, *Newcomb Pottery: An Enterprise for Southern Women, 1895–1940*, Exton, Pa., 1984

Postle, Kathleen R., *The Chronicle of the Overbeck Pottery*, Indianapolis, Ind., 1978

Robineau, Samuel, *Grand Feu Ceramics: A Practical Treatise on the Making of Fine Porcelain and Grès Flammés*, with an introductory essay by Professor Charles F. Binns, Syracuse, N.Y., 1905

The Roycroft Buildings of East Aurora, East Aurora, N.Y., 1973

Roycroft Furniture, firm's catalogue, East Aurora, N.Y., 1906

Spencer, Brian A. *The Prairie School Tradition*, New York, 1979

Stein, Roger, *John Ruskin and Aesthetic Thought in America, 1840–1900*, Cambridge, Mass., 1967

Stott, Mary Roelofs, *Elbert Hubbard: Rebel with Reverence*, New York, 1975

A System of Architectural Ornament According with a Philosophy of Man's Powers, New York, 1924

Trapp, Kenneth R., *Ode to Nature: Flowers and Landscapes of the Rookwood Pottery 1880–1940*, Santa Barbara, Calif., 1980

Weiss, Peg, ed., *Adelaide Alsop Robineau*, Syracuse, N.Y., 1981

Wright, Frank Lloyd, *An Autobiography*, New York 1977
————*A Testament*, New York, 1957

Wright, John Lloyd, *My Father Who Is on Earth*, New York, 1946

Exhibition and Auction Catalogues

The Biloxi Art Pottery of George Ohr, The Mississippi State Historical Museum, 1978

Brandt, Frederick R., *Late 19th and Early 20th Century*

Decorative Arts, The Sydney and Frances Lewis Collection in the Virginia Museum of Fine Arts, Richmond, Va., 1985

Cathers, David M., *Genius in the Shadows: The Furniture Designs of Harvey Ellis*, Jordan-Volpe Gallery, New York, 24 March–2 May 1981

Clark, Robert Judson, ed., *The Arts and Crafts Movement in America 1876–1916*, Princeton, N.J., 1972

The Decorative Designs of Frank Lloyd Wright, The Renwick Gallery, Smithsonian Institution, Washington, D.C., 16 December 1977–30 July 1978

Dietz, Ulysses G., *The Newark Museum Collection of American Art Pottery*, The Newark Museum, Newark, N.J., 1984

Frank Lloyd Wright, Kelmscott Gallery, Chicago, 1981

Frank Lloyd Wright Architectural Drawings and Decorative Art, Fischer Fine Art Ltd, London, 27 June–30 August 1985

Frank Lloyd Wright: A Modern Aesthetic, Struve Gallery, Chicago, 1986

Frank Lloyd Wright and Viollet-le-Duc Organic Architecture and Design from 1850 to 1950, The Armstrong Gallery, New York, 12 March–5 April 1986

Haight, Deborah S., and Blume, Peter F., *Frank Lloyd Wright: The Library from the Francis W. Little House*, Allentown Art Museum, Pennsylvania, 1978

Hanks, David A., *Designs of Frank Lloyd Wright*, Renwick Gallery of the National Collection of Fine Arts, Smithsonian Institution, Washington, D.C., 1978
———and Pierce, Donald C., *The Virginia Carroll Crawford Collection American Decorative Arts, 1825–1917*, High Museum of Art, Atlanta, Ga., 1983

High Fire Porcelains: Adelaide Alsop Robineau Potter, exhibition booklet, the Panama–Pacific Exposition, San Francisco, Calif., 1915

Important American Architectural Designs and Commissions Including Arts and Crafts, auction catalogue, Christie's, New York, 13 June 1986

Important Frank Lloyd Wright and American Arts & Crafts Furnishing Including Ceramics, auction catalogue, Christie's, New York, 12 December 1987

Kaplan, Wendy, *"The Art that is Life": The Arts & Crafts Movement in America, 1875–1920*, Museum of Fine Arts, Boston, 1987

Kaufmann, Edgar, Jr., *Frank Lloyd Wright at the Metropolitan Museum of Art*, museum reprint booklet, Metropolitan Museum of Art, New York, 1982, 1985

Keen, Kirsten Hoving, *American Art Pottery 1875–1930*, Delaware Art Museum, Wilmington, Del., 10 March–23 April 1978

The Roycroft Movement: A Spirit of Today, supplement to an exhibition organized by the Burchfield Center, State University College at Buffalo, 1977

Spencer, Brian A., *The Prairie School Tradition*, Milwaukee Art School, Milwaukee, 1979

Trapp, Kenneth R., *Towards the Modern Style: Rookwood Pottery The Later Years: 1915–1950*, Jordan-Volpe Gallery, New York, 1983

Magazine articles

Clark, Garth, "George E. Ohr," *Antiques Magazine* (September 1985): 496*ff*

Cook, Mary Elizabeth, "Our American Potteries – Weller Ware," *The Sketch Book* (May 1906): 345–46

Crawford, Alan, "Ten Letters from Frank Lloyd Wright to Charles Robert Ashbee," *Architectural History* 13 (1970): 64*ff*

Moffitt, Charlotte, "The Rohlfs Furniture," *House Beautiful* (December 1899): 85*ff*

Rawson, Jonathan A., Jr., "Teco and Robineau Pottery," *House Beautiful* (April 1913): 151*ff*

Rohlfs, Charles, "The Grain of Wood," *House Beautiful* (February 1901): 148*ff*

Ruge, Klara, "Das Kunstgewerbe Amerikas," *Kunst und Kunsthandwerk* 5 (March 1902): 126–48
———"Amerikanische Kunstausstellungen der Saison 1908 bis 1909," *Kunst and Kunsthandwerk* 12 (1909): 562–82
———"Ein Amerikanischer Möbelkünstler Charles Rohlfs Buffalo," *Die Kunst* 4 (1901): 74–79

Wright, Frank Lloyd, "In the Cause of Architecture," *Architectural Record* (July 1928): 16*ff*

Magazines

American Ceramic Society Bulletin 1938–43
Architectural Record 1906–48
Art and Decoration 1900–07
Art Interchange 1896–1902
Art and Progress 1909–11
Art Journal 1897–99
Brush and Pencil 1900–06
Bungalow Magazine 1908–14
The Craftsman 1902–14
Glass and Pottery World 1907–09
Good Housekeeping 1904–11

House Beautiful 1898–1908
House and Garden 1904–11
International Studio 1906–13
Journal of the Society of Architectural Historians 1960–64, 1971
Keramic Studio 1898–1908
Die Kunst 1906
Pencil Points 1924
The Prairie School Review 1964–68
Progressive Architecture 1981–85
Spinning Wheel 1971–72
The Western Architect 1912–14

Index